The Best Ever
Book of
Questions
&
Answers

The Best Ever
Book of
Questions
&
Answers

Written by Ian Graham, Paul Sterry,
and Andrew Langley

Vineyard
BOOKS

Photo Credits

Page 6 (Horsehead Nebula): Royal Observatory, Edinburgh; page 7 (Milky Way): Science Photo Library/Mt Palomar Observatory; page 13 (moonwalk): NASA; page 21 (lightening): Jerome Yeats/Science Photo Library; page 96 (buckle): British Museum, (coin): Hirmer Fotoarchiv, Munich; page 98 (gold clasps): British Museum, London; page 100 (statue): Museum of Mankind, British Museum, London/Michael Holford; page 108 (Hitler, Archduke Franz Ferdinand): Hulton-Deutsch Collection; page 137 (car): Hank Morgan/Science Photo Library.

Specially prepared for
Chapters
90 Ronson Drive
Etobicoke
Ontario M9W 1C1

Planned and produced by
Andromeda Oxford Limited
11-13 The Vineyard
Abingdon, Oxon OX14 3PX
England

ISBN 1-86199-052-9

Printed in Hong Kong by Sing Cheong Printing Co. Ltd.

CONTENTS

MYSTERIOUS UNIVERSE

Q How did the Sun and planets form?

A Nobody knows for sure. Most scientists think that the Sun, Earth, and other planets (the solar system) were formed from a mass of dust and gas. Nearly 5 billion years ago, this mass started to shrink, and then spin and flatten into a disk. The center of the disk spun fastest. This became the Sun. The rest of the material turned into the planets (below).

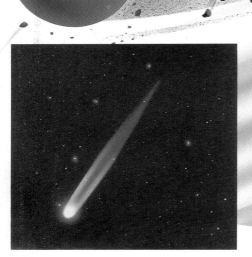

Q What is a meteor?

A A meteor is a sudden streak of light in the sky (above). It is caused by a piece of rock from outer space entering the Earth's atmosphere. The friction causes it to burn up.

Q What is a nebula?

A A nebula is a cloud of dust and gas in space. Some of the clouds block the light from the stars behind them. These are called dark nebulae. One of the best-known is the Horsehead Nebula (right). Other dust clouds reflect the light from the stars and shine brightly. These are called bright nebulae.

Q What is a black hole?

A Sometimes – no one knows why – stars collapse in on themselves. This increases their gravity (a force that pulls everything inward). Nothing escapes – not even light. These very dense bodies are called black holes (below).

Q What is a galaxy?

A A galaxy (below) is a huge spinning mass of stars in outer space. There are millions of galaxies, each containing billions of stars plus gas and dust. Our galaxy is called the Milky Way. It contains about 200 billion stars.

Q How did the universe begin?

A Many scientists believe that all the material of the universe was once crammed together in one place. Then, about 15 billion years ago, an explosion or "Big Bang" occurred. The material of the universe flew out in all directions, forming galaxies and other bodies, mainly gas and dust. The effects of this explosion are still continuing, causing the universe to expand (right). The galaxies still seem to be rushing away from each other.

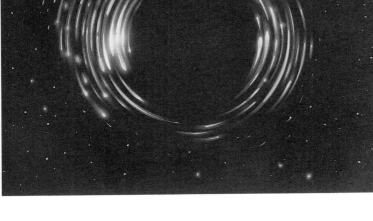

Galaxies

SOLAR SYSTEM

Cameras

UHF antenna

Digging arm

Footpad

Altitude in km

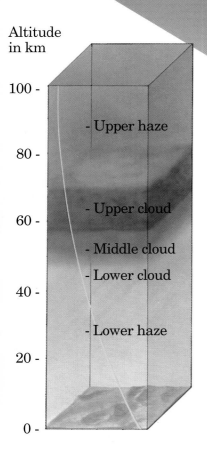

100 -

80 -

- Upper haze

60 -

- Upper cloud

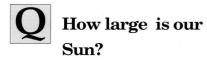
- Middle cloud

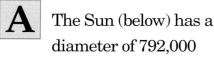
- Lower cloud

40 -

- Lower haze

20 -

0 -

Q **Which is the hottest planet?**

A Venus. It is the second planet from the Sun. Venus is completely covered in dense clouds (left). These act like a giant greenhouse, raising temperatures to 863.6 °F. Several probes have landed on Venus, but none has survived.

Q **Is there life on Mars?**

A In 1976 two Viking probes (above) landed on Mars and sent pictures of the rocky surface back to Earth. There were no astronauts aboard the Viking probes, so automatic soil samplers tested the red, dry soil for any sign of life. None was found.

Q **Which planets have rings?**

A Jupiter, Saturn, Uranus, and Neptune have rings. The rings are actually tiny pieces of rock covered with ice. Rings may be fragments of moons that were destroyed, or they may have been part of the planets.

Q **How large is our Sun?**

A The Sun (below) has a diameter of 792,000 miles. Its volume is approximately 1.3 million times larger than the Earth's. However, the Sun is only a medium-sized star; many stars are much bigger. By comparison, the biggest planet in our solar system is Jupiter (85,800 miles diameter), and the smallest is Pluto (1,200 miles diameter).

Jupiter

Mercury

Venus

Earth

Mars

Sun

Q How hot is the Sun?

A The Sun is a vast ball of glowing gas (right). At the heart of the Sun, temperatures are thought to be 27,000,000 °F! The heat is created in the core, or center, by the nuclear fusion of hydrogen atoms. This is similar to the process that occurs in an exploding hydrogen bomb. Marks on the Sun, called sunspots, appear dark only because they are 2,200 °F. cooler than the surrounding gas. Solar flares are great tongues of gas. All life on Earth is dependent on the light and heat from the Sun.

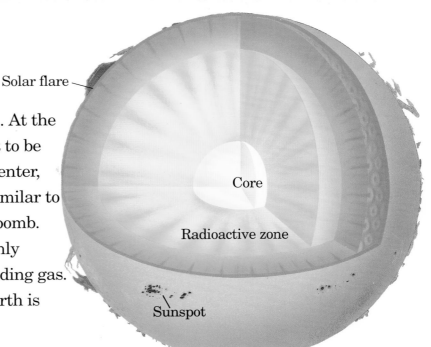

Solar flare

Core

Radioactive zone

Sunspot

Q How do we know so much about the planets?

A Space probes travel through the solar system sending information back to Earth. Space probes carry cameras to take pictures, along with equipment to detect the presence of radio waves and magnetic fields.

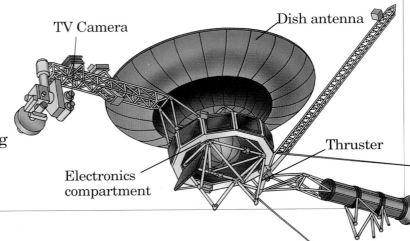

TV Camera

Dish antenna

Thruster

Electronics compartment

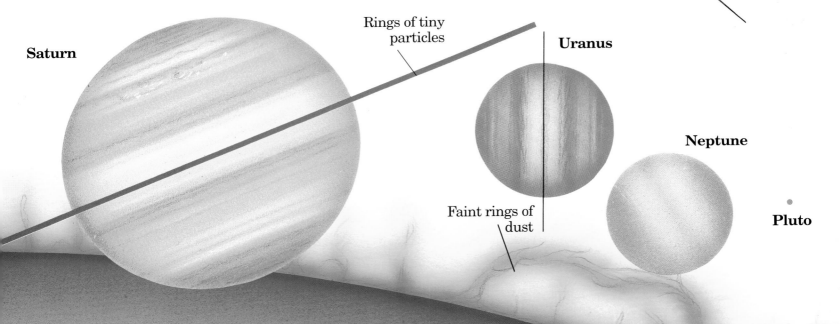

Saturn

Rings of tiny particles

Uranus

Neptune

Faint rings of dust

Pluto

These are the planets of our Sun, with their sizes drawn to scale. The distances between them are not drawn to scale.

SPACE

THE PLANETS

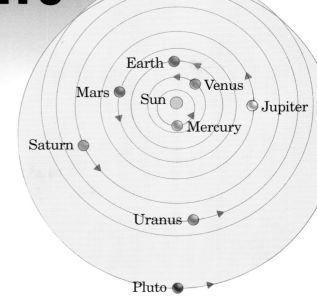

Q What are planets made of?

A The planets that are closest to the Sun, from Mercury to Mars, are small, rocky worlds. They have a metal center, or core, surrounded by a thick mantle of rock with a thin, rocky crust on the surface. The outer planets are very different. Jupiter and Saturn are made mostly of hydrogen. Uranus and Neptune have a rocky core surrounded by ice and hydrogen (below). Pluto is made of rock, with an icy coating.

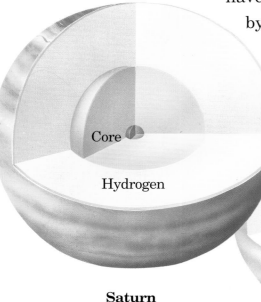

Saturn

Uranus

Q How do the planets orbit the Sun?

A All the planets in the solar system travel in the same direction around the Sun (above). Their paths are slightly flattened circles called ellipses. Pluto's orbit is pushed so far to one side that it crosses Neptune's orbit.

Q What are planets?

A Planets are worlds that orbit the Sun. The word "planet" comes from a Greek word meaning wanderer, because of the strange wandering paths they appear to have when seen from Earth. There are nine planets (right). Mercury is the closest to the Sun, then Venus, Earth, Mars, Jupiter, Saturn, Uranus, Neptune, and Pluto.

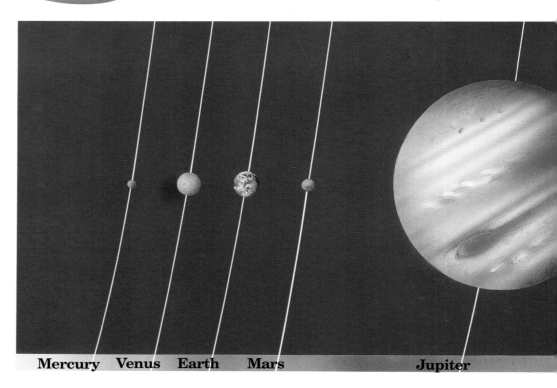

Mercury   Venus   Earth   Mars   Jupiter

 What is the Great Red Spot?

 Jupiter's Great Red Spot (below) is a swirling storm 18,600 miles across. It was first seen by astronomers as long ago as 1664. Storms on Earth last a few weeks at most. The Great Red Spot has lasted for centuries because Jupiter has no solid surface to slow it down.

Great Red Spot

 Which planets have moons?

 Only Mercury and Venus do not have moons. Earth has one moon. Mars has two (above). Jupiter has 16 moons. One of them, Ganymede, is larger than the planet Mercury. Saturn has 19 moons, Uranus 17, Neptune eight while Pluto has only one.

 What are the canals of Mars?

 Over the centuries, astronomers thought that the dark lines and patches on the surface of Mars might be canals, built by an ancient civilization for carrying water. However, none of these so-called canals are visible in photographs taken by probes sent from Earth to Mars. Therefore scientists now believe that the canals are probably an optical illusion.

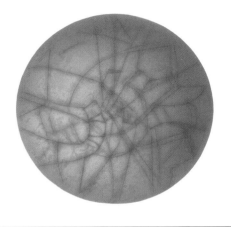

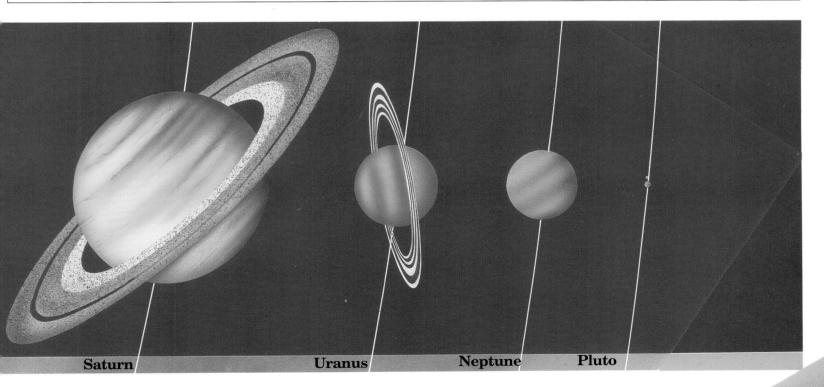

Saturn   **Uranus**   **Neptune**   **Pluto**

MOON

Q Why does the Moon seem to change shape?

A The Moon shines because it reflects light from the Sun. However, as it travels around the Earth, we see more or less of its surface, making it appear to change in shape. The different shapes are called phases (below).

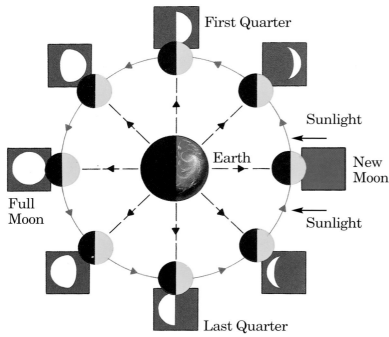

First Quarter

Sunlight

Earth

New Moon

Full Moon

Sunlight

Last Quarter

Q What is inside the Moon?

A No one has ever examined the inside of the Moon (below). Its outside looks very different from the Earth, but inside it is probably the same. Beneath the thin outer crust is a mantle of solid rock. Under this is a thinner layer of molten rock, and at the center is the core, about 880 miles from the surface.

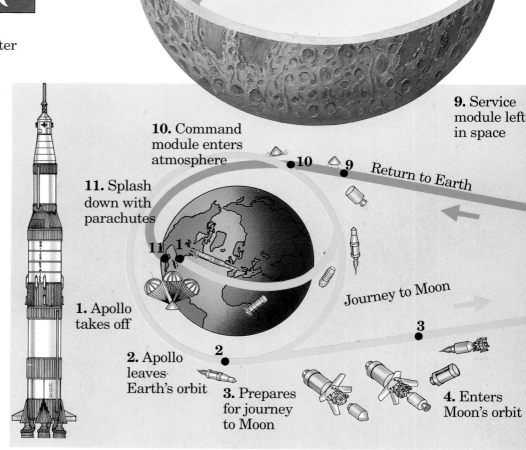

40 mi.

600 mi.

215 mi.

185 mi.

Crust

Core

Molten Rock

Mantle

Q When did people first land on the Moon?

A The Apollo 11 spacecraft (right) took off in July 1969. It was carried by a huge Saturn rocket for the first stage of its journey. Shooting out of Earth's orbit, Apollo traveled to the Moon. The lunar module separated and landed on the Moon's surface. Two of the crew, Neil Armstrong and Edwin Aldrin, became the first people to walk on the Moon.

9. Service module left in space

10. Command module enters atmosphere

11. Splash down with parachutes

Return to Earth

1. Apollo takes off

2. Apollo leaves Earth's orbit

3. Prepares for journey to Moon

Journey to Moon

4. Enters Moon's orbit

SPACE

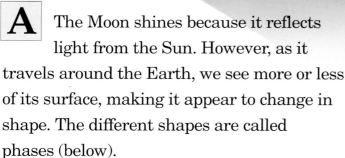

Q What is on the surface of the Moon?

A The Moon's surface (right) is covered with dust and rocks that have been smashed to pieces by showers of rocklike objects called meteorites. It is pitted with craters, also caused by meteorites. Most are just tiny dents, but some are hundreds of miles wide. Some areas of the Moon look dark. People once thought these areas were seas. They were formed when meteorites cracked the Moon's surface. Molten rock bubbled up from below and grew hard. There are also many high mountains and deep valleys.

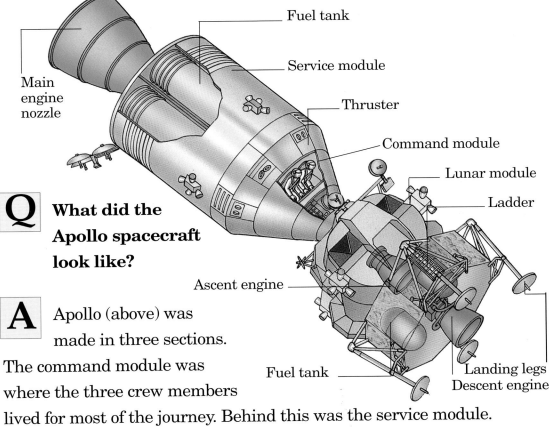

Fuel tank

Service module

Thruster

Command module

Lunar module

Ladder

Main engine nozzle

Ascent engine

Fuel tank

Landing legs

Descent engine

Q What did the Apollo spacecraft look like?

A Apollo (above) was made in three sections. The command module was where the three crew members lived for most of the journey. Behind this was the service module. This contained the rocket engine and tanks for fuel and oxygen. The lunar module was used for landing on the Moon. It had four legs that spread out to support it on the Moon's surface. The lunar module and service module were left behind in space. Only the command module returned to splash down in the Pacific Ocean.

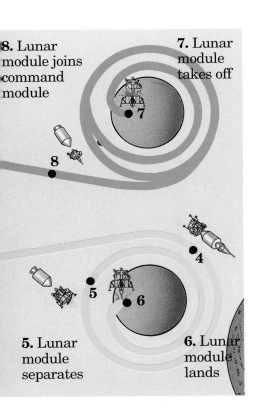

8. Lunar module joins command module

7. Lunar module takes off

● 7

● 8

● 4

● 5

● 6

5. Lunar module separates

6. Lunar module lands

EXPLORING THE HEAVENS

Q How did early astronomers study the heavens?

A Astronomers studied the sky with the naked eye until the 17th century. In 1609 the Italian astronomer Galileo Galilei (above) became the first person to study the sky with a telescope.

Q What did Giotto tell us about comets?

A In 1986, the Giotto space probe (below) studied Halley's Comet. A comet consists of a lump of rock and ice called the nucleus, inside a cloud of gas and dust called the coma (inset). It also has a bright tail. Giotto's photographs show a nucleus measuring 5 miles by 7.5 miles. Its instruments found that the coma and tail are made of dust and water vapor.

Q How does a modern telescope work?

A There are two types of telescope. A refractor uses a lens to form an image. A reflector uses a curved mirror. Most modern telescopes used in astronomy are reflectors. The telescope is finely balanced and turns slowly to keep the image steady as the Earth moves. A Schmidt telescope (right) is used to photograph large areas of the sky.

Schmidt telescope gathering light from the stars

Counterbalance

Inside the telescope

Mirror

Light rays

Eyepiece

Q Why is the Hubble Telescope in space?

A Light from distant stars passes through the Earth's atmosphere before it reaches a telescope on the ground. The swirling atmosphere makes the stars twinkle. Modern telescopes are usually built on top of mountains, where the atmosphere is thinner, to reduce this effect. The Hubble Space Telescope (below) can see more clearly than any telescope on Earth because it is above the atmosphere.

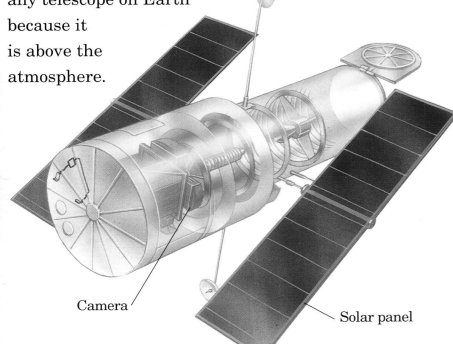

Camera

Solar panel

Q How did the Pioneer space probes work?

A Pioneer 10 and 11 (right) were the first spacecraft to visit the outer solar system. They were designed to find out if a spacecraft could travel through the asteroid belt, a swarm of rocks orbiting the Sun between Mars and Jupiter. Most spacecraft use solar cells to make electricity from sunlight. Pioneer 10 and 11 traveled so far from the Sun that solar cells would not work. Instead, they carried nuclear power generators to make electricity.

Thruster

Nuclear power generator

Cosmic ray telescope

Q Where did the Voyager space probes go?

A Voyager 1 and 2 were launched in 1977. The pull of gravity from the outer planets guided the spacecraft from one planet to the next. Voyager 1 flew past Jupiter in 1979 (below) and Saturn in 1980. Voyager 2 flew past Jupiter (1979), Saturn (1981), Uranus (1986), and Neptune (1989). Their cameras and instruments studied each planet. All the information was sent back to Earth by radio.

Pioneer 11

SPACE TRAVEL

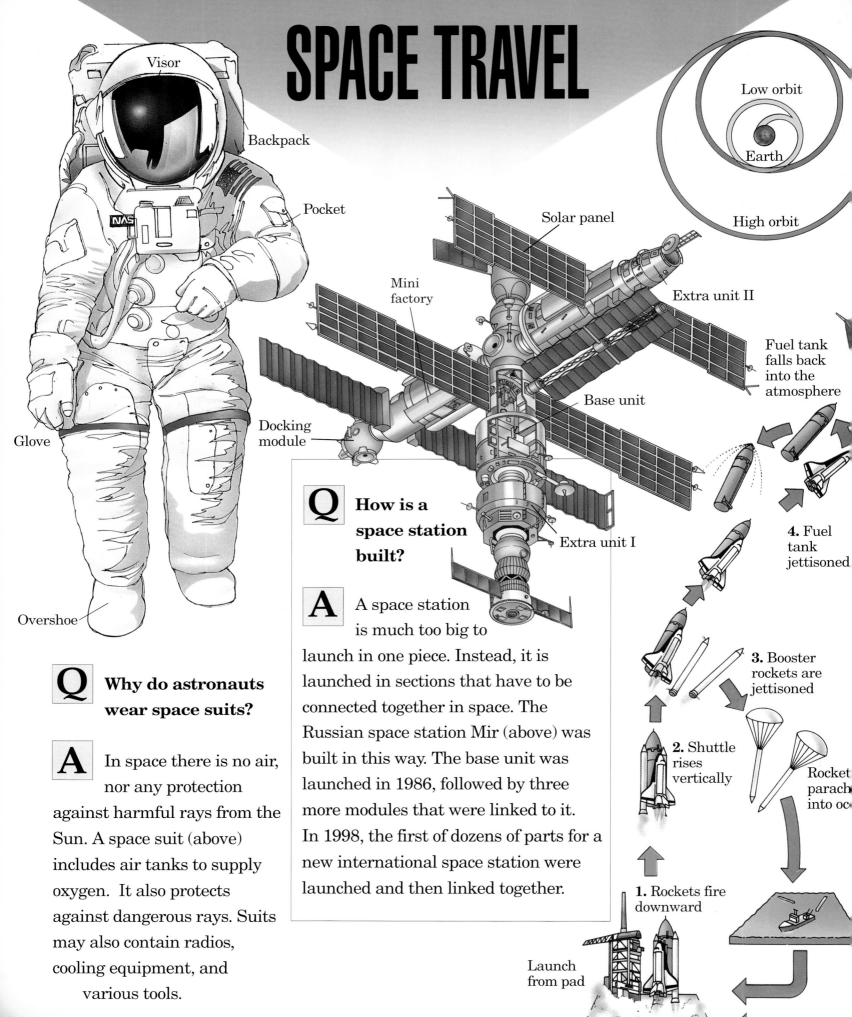

Visor

Backpack

Pocket

NASA

Glove

Overshoe

Low orbit

Earth

High orbit

Solar panel

Mini factory

Extra unit II

Fuel tank falls back into the atmosphere

Base unit

Docking module

Extra unit I

Q How is a space station built?

A A space station is much too big to launch in one piece. Instead, it is launched in sections that have to be connected together in space. The Russian space station Mir (above) was built in this way. The base unit was launched in 1986, followed by three more modules that were linked to it. In 1998, the first of dozens of parts for a new international space station were launched and then linked together.

4. Fuel tank jettisoned

3. Booster rockets are jettisoned

2. Shuttle rises vertically

Rocket parach into oc

Q Why do astronauts wear space suits?

A In space there is no air, nor any protection against harmful rays from the Sun. A space suit (above) includes air tanks to supply oxygen. It also protects against dangerous rays. Suits may also contain radios, cooling equipment, and various tools.

1. Rockets fire downward

Launch from pad

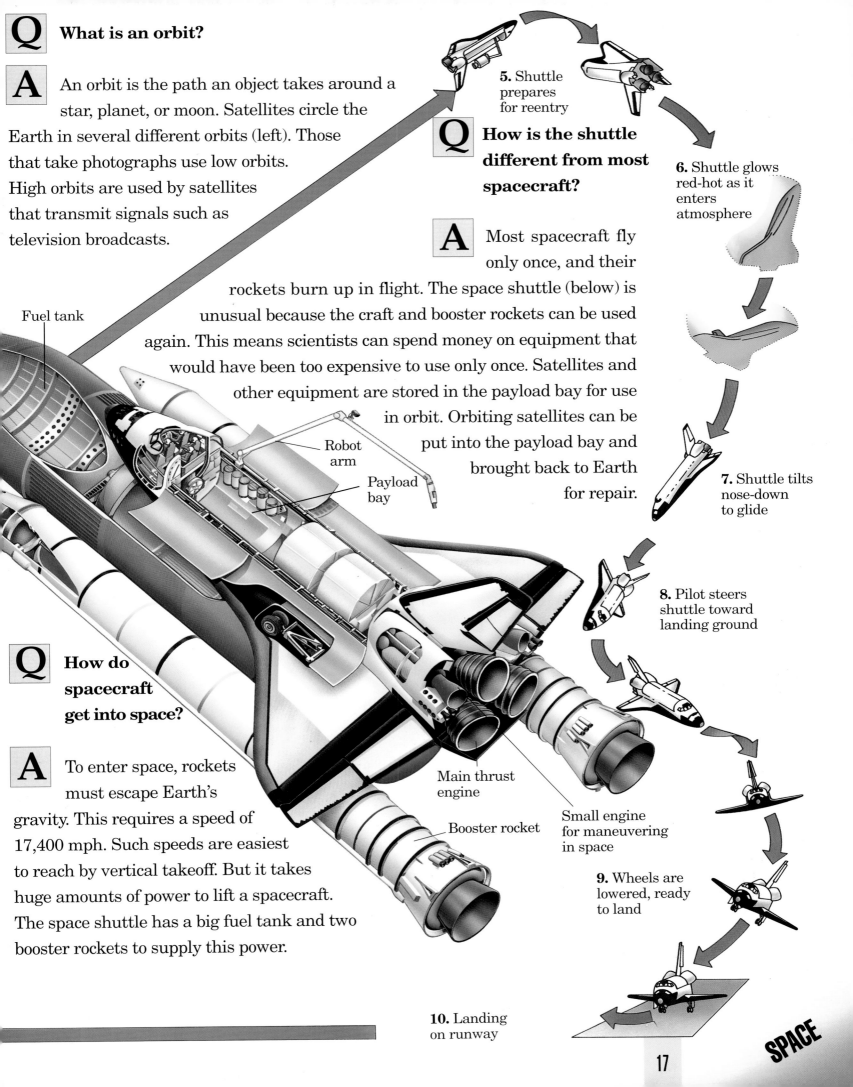

Q What is an orbit?

A An orbit is the path an object takes around a star, planet, or moon. Satellites circle the Earth in several different orbits (left). Those that take photographs use low orbits. High orbits are used by satellites that transmit signals such as television broadcasts.

Fuel tank

Robot arm

Payload bay

Q How do spacecraft get into space?

A To enter space, rockets must escape Earth's gravity. This requires a speed of 17,400 mph. Such speeds are easiest to reach by vertical takeoff. But it takes huge amounts of power to lift a spacecraft. The space shuttle has a big fuel tank and two booster rockets to supply this power.

Main thrust engine

Booster rocket

Small engine for maneuvering in space

5. Shuttle prepares for reentry

Q How is the shuttle different from most spacecraft?

A Most spacecraft fly only once, and their rockets burn up in flight. The space shuttle (below) is unusual because the craft and booster rockets can be used again. This means scientists can spend money on equipment that would have been too expensive to use only once. Satellites and other equipment are stored in the payload bay for use in orbit. Orbiting satellites can be put into the payload bay and brought back to Earth for repair.

6. Shuttle glows red-hot as it enters atmosphere

7. Shuttle tilts nose-down to glide

8. Pilot steers shuttle toward landing ground

9. Wheels are lowered, ready to land

10. Landing on runway

SPACE

17

PLANET EARTH

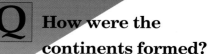

 What is inside the Earth?

A The thin outer layer of the Earth (below) is called the crust. Beneath this is the solid mantle that makes up most of the Earth. The mantle is a mixture of rocks and minerals. Right at the center of the Earth is the core of molten iron and nickel. The inner part of the core may be as hot as 11,700 °F.

Q **How were the continents formed?**

A Scientists believe that the continents (below) were formed from one giant landmass they call Pangaea. This broke in two, then split up into smaller landmasses. These drifted apart until they reached their present places. But they are still moving!

286–248 million years ago

213–144 million years ago

65–25 million years ago

400 mi.

1,400 mi.

1,400 mi.

750 mi.

Lower mantle

Outer core

Inner core

Upper mantle

Crust

Q Why do we have seasons?

A The Earth takes one year to move around the Sun. But the Earth is tilted on its axis. This means that different parts of the Earth receive different amounts of sunlight, and so become warmer or colder as the Earth travels on its journey. When the North Pole is nearest the Sun, the northern part of the Earth is warmest. Here it is summer. At the same time, the southern part is tilted away from the Sun, and is cooler. Here it is winter.

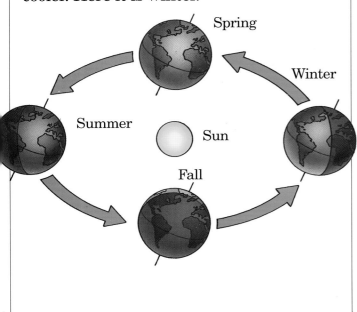

Spring

Winter

Summer

Sun

Fall

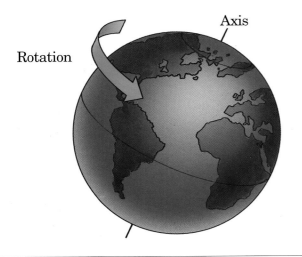

Axis

Rotation

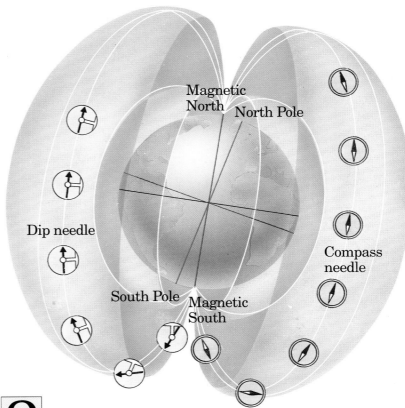

Magnetic North

North Pole

Dip needle

Compass needle

South Pole

Magnetic South

Q Why does a compass needle point north?

A The Earth is like a huge magnet with a force field that covers its whole surface (above). The poles of the magnet are near the North and South Poles. Magnetized objects – such as compass needles – are drawn to these poles. Therefore one end of a compass needle will always point north.

Q What were the ice ages?

A The ice ages (right) were periods in history when the Earth became extremely cold. The last ice age ended about 10,000 years ago. Near the poles, a lot of water froze into ice. This meant that there was less water in the sea and the sea level dropped, leaving large areas of land uncovered.

Earth during ice age

Earth today

OUR WORLD

NATURAL FORCES

Gas, ash, and rock fragments

Lava

Layers of lava and ash

Crater left by previous eruption

Q What is a hurricane?

A A hurricane is a very strong whirling storm (right). The winds near the center can reach 155 mph. Hurricanes begin over warm tropical seas. The surface water heats up and evaporates to form clouds. This releases the heat and makes the clouds rise. Air is sucked in from the surrounding area, swirling the clouds into a spiral. At the very center of the hurricane is a calm area called the eye. As hurricanes move, they push the sea into huge waves and may cause floods. When the hurricane reaches land, it slowly grows weaker. But the high winds can still cause great damage to buildings and trees.

Q Why do volcanoes erupt?

A Volcanoes erupt when hot molten rock from inside the Earth forces its way through cracks in the Earth's surface (above left). This rock, called lava, flows from the volcano and cools.

Q What is a seismograph?

A A seismograph measures earthquakes. When an earthquake occurs, its hanging arm shakes, and the pen marks the paper on the revolving drum.

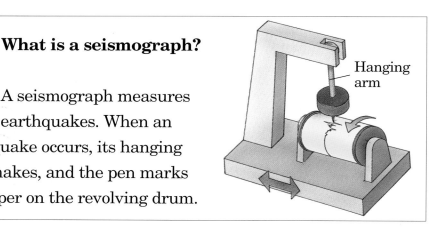

Hanging arm

Q How do we measure wind speed?

A The speed of the wind is measured on the Beaufort Scale. This goes from 0 (calm) to 12 (hurricane). The scale describes how things behave at different wind speeds (right). At 1, light air, smoke drifts slowly. At Force 6, large trees sway, and at Force 10, buildings may be damaged.

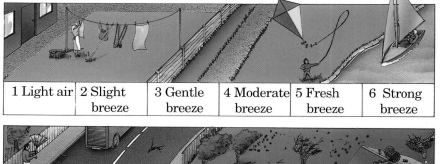

| 1 Light air | 2 Slight breeze | 3 Gentle breeze | 4 Moderate breeze | 5 Fresh breeze | 6 Strong breeze |

| 7 High wind | 8 Gale | 9 Strong gale | 10 Whole gale | 11 Storm | 12 Hurricane |

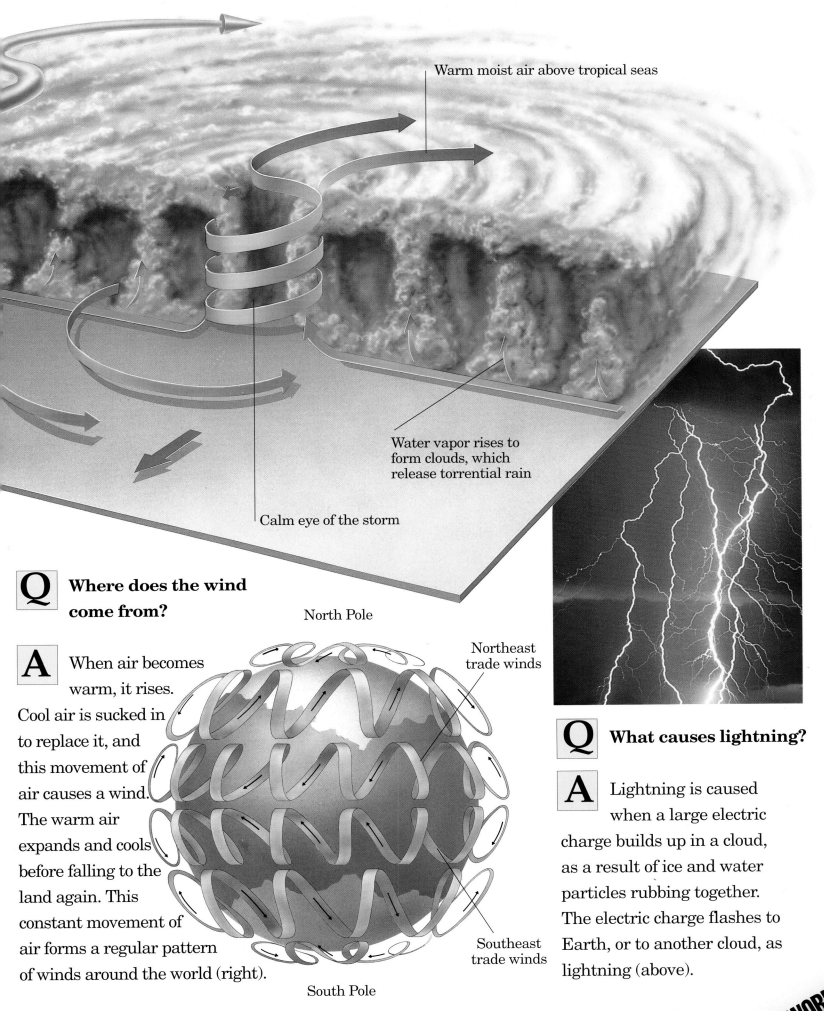

Warm moist air above tropical seas

Water vapor rises to form clouds, which release torrential rain

Calm eye of the storm

North Pole

Northeast trade winds

Southeast trade winds

South Pole

Q **Where does the wind come from?**

A When air becomes warm, it rises. Cool air is sucked in to replace it, and this movement of air causes a wind. The warm air expands and cools before falling to the land again. This constant movement of air forms a regular pattern of winds around the world (right).

Q **What causes lightning?**

A Lightning is caused when a large electric charge builds up in a cloud, as a result of ice and water particles rubbing together. The electric charge flashes to Earth, or to another cloud, as lightning (above).

OUR WORLD

WATER

Q What lies under the oceans?

A The sea floor (below) has plains, valleys, mountains, and even volcanoes. Near the shore is the shallow continental shelf. This slopes to the plain, about 13,000 feet below. On the plain are deep cracks called ocean trenches, and raised areas called ridges.

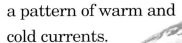

Q How much of the Earth is covered by oceans?

A The oceans cover 71 percent of the Earth. The continents are actually huge islands in a continuous stretch of water (below). The water flows around the world in a pattern of warm and cold currents.

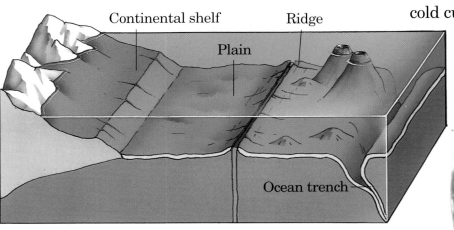

Continental shelf   Ridge

Plain

Ocean trench

Q How does the sea change the coastline?

A The waves of the sea constantly pound the edge of the land (right). They change the shape of the coastline in two ways. First, the waves smash against the rocks and grind them into pebbles and sand. They hurl the pebbles at the cliffs, slowly wearing them away. But the sea also moves the sand and pebbles to other places. Beaches are formed, and the coastline is built up where the sea drops them.

Waves wear away cliffs

Waves grind down pebbles to form sand

Q What is the water cycle?

A Water is always on the move (right), changing from liquid to vapor and back to liquid. The heat of the Sun evaporates water from the oceans, lakes, and rivers. Plants also release moisture from their leaves. The moisture rises into the air and cools to form clouds. Winds blow the clouds toward the land. Here the clouds grow cooler, especially over high ground, and it starts to rain. The rain drains into rivers and lakes and then back into the sea.

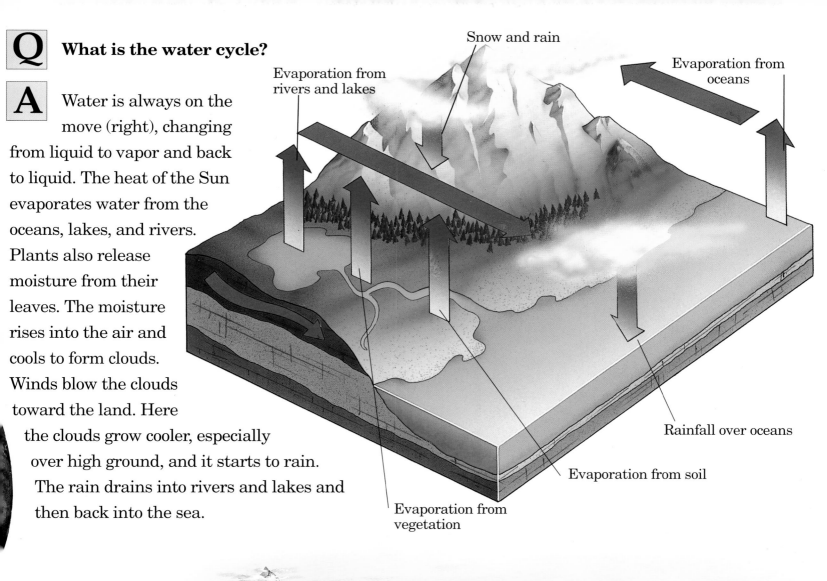

Snow and rain

Evaporation from oceans

Evaporation from rivers and lakes

Rainfall over oceans

Evaporation from soil

Evaporation from vegetation

Q What is a glacier?

A A glacier (right) is a river of ice that forms in cold regions high up in the mountains or near the poles. It slides very slowly downhill, a few feet each year. It carries a mass of rocks, which scrape away the valley walls and floor. It later deposits rocks and earth in huge ridges called moraines. If a glacier reaches the sea, large pieces break off and float away as icebergs.

Icefall

Arête, a narrow ridge left between glaciers

Avalanche

Moraine

OUR WORLD

LANDSCAPE

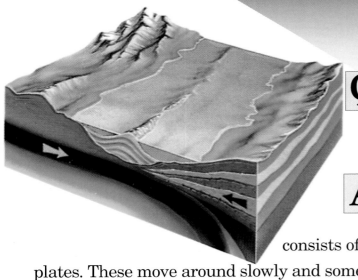

Q **How are mountains made?**

A The surface of the Earth consists of a series of huge plates. These move around slowly and sometimes collide with each other (above). When this happens, the edges of the plates are pushed up and the layers of rock crumple and fold. Over millions of years, the folds form chains of mountains.

Q **How are caves formed?**

A Many caves are found in limestone rock (below). They are formed when rainwater soaks down through cracks in the rock. The water dissolves the limestone, making the cracks bigger. Now streams can flow in underground. They wear away weak parts of the rock to make caves. Sometimes water drips into the caves. The dissolved limestone forms hanging spikes called stalactites. Pillars called stalagmites form on the floor below.

Q **What is soil made of?**

A Soil is a mixture of rock particles and humus, which is made up of the tissues of dead plants and animals. The humus breaks down and releases minerals which help plants grow. Below the soil is the rocky subsoil, and beneath that the solid rock known as bedrock.

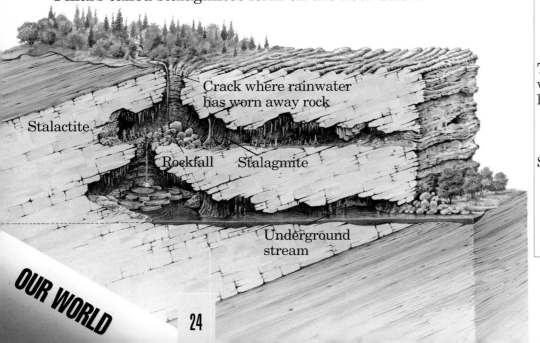

Crack where rainwater has worn away rock

Stalactite

Rockfall   Stalagmite

Underground stream

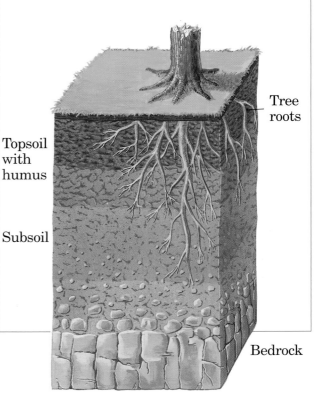

Tree roots

Topsoil with humus

Subsoil

Bedrock

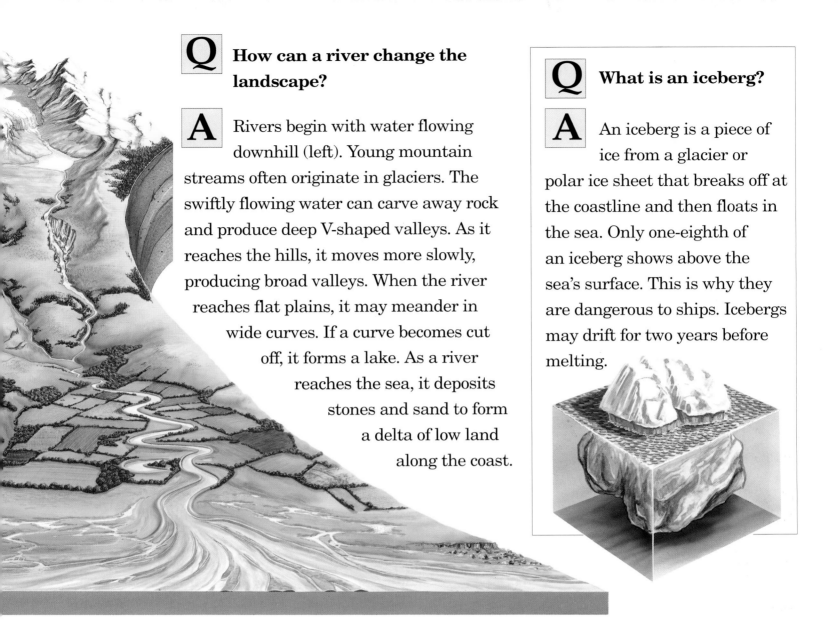

Q How can a river change the landscape?

A Rivers begin with water flowing downhill (left). Young mountain streams often originate in glaciers. The swiftly flowing water can carve away rock and produce deep V-shaped valleys. As it reaches the hills, it moves more slowly, producing broad valleys. When the river reaches flat plains, it may meander in wide curves. If a curve becomes cut off, it forms a lake. As a river reaches the sea, it deposits stones and sand to form a delta of low land along the coast.

Q What is an iceberg?

A An iceberg is a piece of ice from a glacier or polar ice sheet that breaks off at the coastline and then floats in the sea. Only one-eighth of an iceberg shows above the sea's surface. This is why they are dangerous to ships. Icebergs may drift for two years before melting.

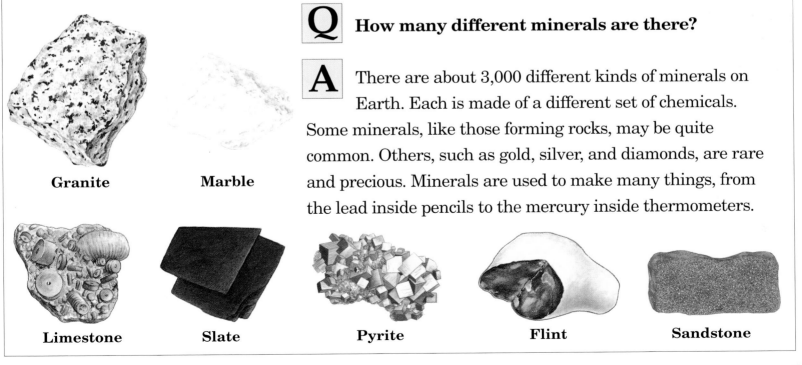

Q How many different minerals are there?

A There are about 3,000 different kinds of minerals on Earth. Each is made of a different set of chemicals. Some minerals, like those forming rocks, may be quite common. Others, such as gold, silver, and diamonds, are rare and precious. Minerals are used to make many things, from the lead inside pencils to the mercury inside thermometers.

Granite

Marble

Limestone

Slate

Pyrite

Flint

Sandstone

Q What causes the winds?

A Winds are created because of differences in air temperature and air pressure. When air is heated at the equator (below), it rises, cools, and then sinks over the tropics. Some air moves back again toward the equator, creating the trade winds. The rest is drawn toward the poles as westerly winds.

Earth's rotation

Polar jet streams

Westerly winds

Equator

Trade winds

Subtropical jet streams

Water vapor in clouds

Water falls as rain

Q How are clouds formed?

A Water evaporates from land, lakes, and sea (above) and is carried by the air as water vapor. Warm air can hold more water vapor than cold air. As warm air rises and cools, for example over a mountain, the water vapor condenses to water, forming clouds. Eventually, the water falls from the clouds as rain. The rainwater runs back into the rivers and lakes.

Q What is erosion?

A Erosion is the breaking down of solid rock into smaller particles, which are then carried away. Wind, water, gravity, sea, and rain are common natural causes of erosion, and so is ice (below). The frozen ice in the glacier carves U-shaped valleys as it moves slowly downhill. Most mountain valleys are formed in this way. Today, human activity also causes damaging erosion.

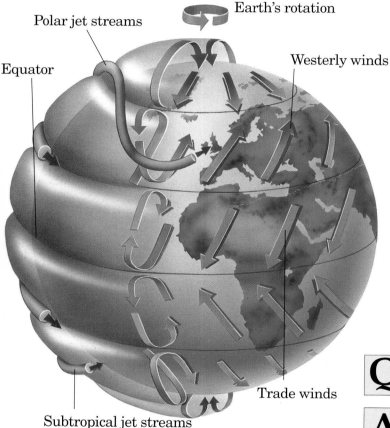

Ice

Water

Gravity

Wind

Sea

Q What is energy conservation?

A We use a lot of energy in our homes. Much of it comes from oil, coal, or gas, which are fossil fuels that will one day be used up. If we insulate our houses better, and trap the Sun's heat, we use less fuel. This is called energy conservation. We can also use everlasting energy sources, such as wind (below).

Wind-powered generator

Solar panel

Heat insulation

Water-powered generator

Methane generator

Q Why is pollution harmful?

A Many of the fumes and chemicals produced by cars or industry (below) can damage plants and animals. Even small amounts of some polluting gases or liquids can kill large numbers of living things, and many are also poisonous to people as well.

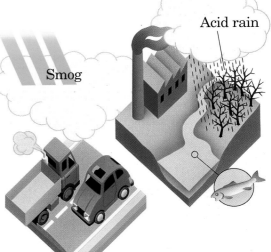

Acid rain

Smog

Q How does the peppered moth adapt to pollution?

A The peppered moth rests on tree bark, where its camouflage hides it from bird predators. The bark in polluted cities may be black, and normal camouflage would be useless. In these areas, a black-winged form of the moth is found.

Normal form　　**Black-winged form**

Q What is deforestation?

A Forests once covered 15 billion acres of the Earth but now only 10 billion acres are left (below). The process of cutting down trees is called deforestation, and is carried out by people. Trees are important to our survival because, like other green plants, they produce oxygen. Without oxygen, animals, including humans, cannot survive.

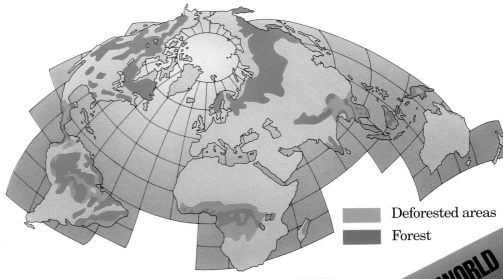

Deforested areas
Forest

HABITATS

Q What is succession?

A Succession is the natural process by which habitats change, and one community of plants and animals is slowly replaced by another. The picture below shows an example of succession at work as a temperate lake silts up, and the dry land eventually becomes oak woodland.

Beaver's lodge

50 years

20 years

10 years

After 5 years

Lake

Plankton

Q Can animals change a habitat?

A Some animals can change their habitats. Beavers cut down trees with their strong teeth. Then they use the trees, together with mud and stones, to dam streams. Their homes, called lodges, are large piles of sticks built up from the bottom of the ponds they have created (above). Here, they raise their young, safely away from predators.

Q What is a habitat?

A A habitat is a place where plants and animals live together as a community. Most creatures only live in one type of habitat, and cannot survive elsewhere. Look at the different habitats seen (right) in the picture of an ocean. Most life is found near the surface. A few species of fish and squid live in deeper water. The seabed is the realm of specially adapted marine creatures that cannot survive elsewhere in the ocean.

Shark

Dolph

Bluefin tuna

Giant squid

Deep-sea jellyfish

Ska

Anglerfish

Q What are the world's main land habitats?

A The world's land habitats range from cold tundra and mountains, through hot deserts and grasslands, to the temperate woods and tropical rain forests, teeming with life. The ten major habitats are shown below. Each has its own type of climate, and plant and animal life.

Q How do wading birds avoid competing for food?

A These wading birds all have specially shaped beaks for catching different creatures on the seashore. So, even though they live in the same habitat, they do not compete for food.

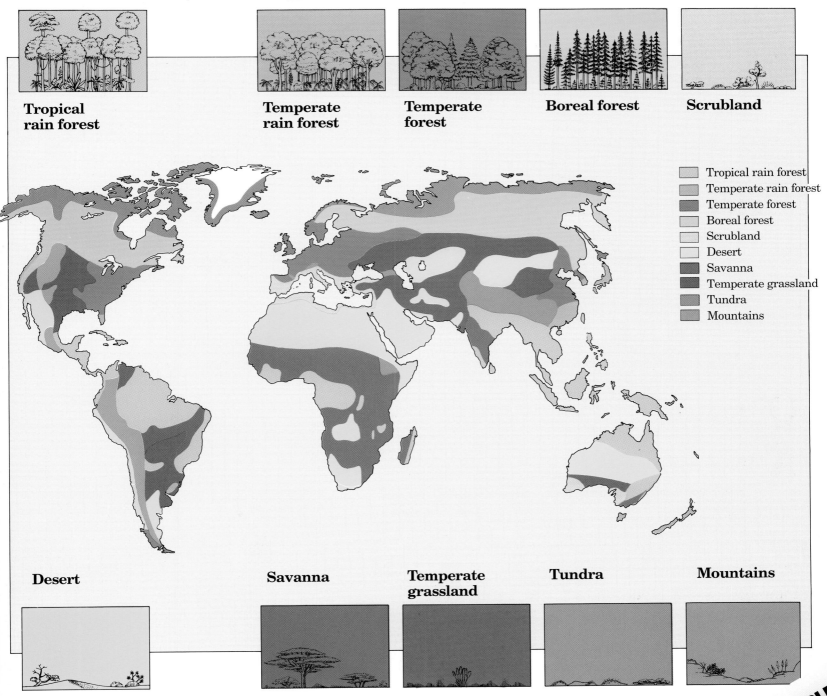

Flamingo
Shelduck
Avocet
Stilt
Golden plover
Kentish plover
Oystercatcher

Tropical rain forest

Temperate rain forest

Temperate forest

Boreal forest

Scrubland

Tropical rain forest
Temperate rain forest
Temperate forest
Boreal forest
Scrubland
Desert
Savanna
Temperate grassland
Tundra
Mountains

Desert

Savanna

Temperate grassland

Tundra

Mountains

HABITATS

Q What lives in a habitat?

A A habitat is a particular place, such as a woodland or a pond. Certain plants and animals are suited to living there, and nowhere else. They have adapted to living in that habitat. In this pond scene (below), the fish and plants can only live in the water, not on dry land. Birds such as herons and swans only feed and nest in watery habitats.

Q What is an endangered species?

A An endangered species is one that is rare and threatened with extinction. The manatee has become rare because of hunting and pollution. The koala's woodland habitat is under threat, while the kakapo, a New Zealand parrot, has been hunted, and is now killed by rats and cats.

Koala

Kakapo

Manatee

Q How do habitats change?

A Although people change habitats, the process also happens naturally. This cross section through a pond (right) shows the gradual process of filling-in. Over the years, the roots of the water plants trap silt, so the pond holds less and less water. The pond becomes silted up and will eventually become dry land.

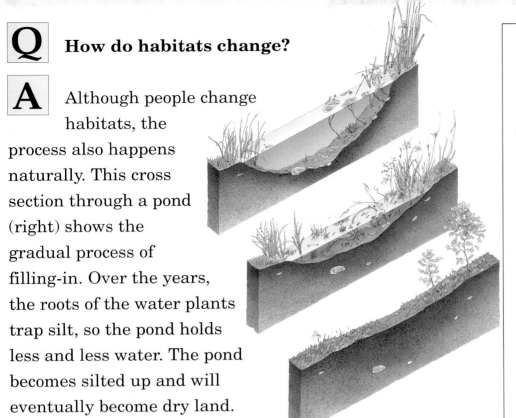

Q What is a food web?

A A food web (below) is a way of showing how plants and animals in a habitat depend on each other. The arrows show which species provide food for other species. Some of the small animals are food for a number of larger predators.

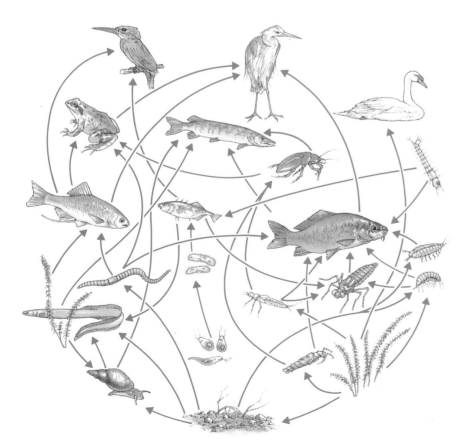

Q How do animals adapt to changes in their environment?

A In many parts of the world the environment changes with the seasons. When winter comes, some animals hibernate and others migrate. The arctic hare has adapted to winter snowfall by shedding its brown summer coat for a white winter one. This gives it camouflage throughout the year.

Q What is a microhabitat?

A Every habitat contains lots of smaller habitats called microhabitats. The creatures that live there are specially adapted to its conditions. These mites, for example, can only survive among particles of soil.

WORLD FACTS

Q Which is the world's largest country?

A Russia has an area of 6,592,800 square miles, making it the world's largest country. The second largest country is Canada, with an area of 3,849,675 square miles. Close behind it is China, with an area of 3,696,100 square miles.

Q Where is the biggest freshwater lake in the world?

A A lake is a large area of water surrounded by land. The biggest freshwater lake is Lake Superior in North America, which stretches for 31,700 square miles. Some of the largest lakes are actually seas, full of salt water. These include the Caspian Sea and the Aral Sea.

Q Which place has the least rain?

A The world receives an average of 34 inches of rain, snow, and hail each year. But some places get little or no rain at all. The driest place in the world is Arica in Chile, which receives less than a tenth of one millimeter of rain a year. In parts of West Africa and South America, rain falls nearly every day.

Q Which is the biggest island in the world?

A Greenland is by far the world's biggest island, at 840,000 square miles.

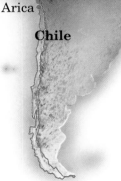

Greenland

Canada

NORTH AMERICA

Lake Superior

U.S.A.

ATLANTIC OCEAN

Saha

PACIFIC OCEAN

SOUTH AMERICA

Arica

Chile

ANTARCTIC OCEAN

Q Which is the world's smallest country?

A Vatican City is the world's smallest country. It covers only 110 acres and lies inside another city – Rome, in Italy. Yet it is an independent state, with its own bank, railroad station, and postage stamps. It is the center of the Roman Catholic Church.

Q Which is the largest desert in the world?

A A desert is a hot, dry region where there is low rainfall and little can grow. By far the biggest desert region is the Sahara in North Africa. This covers over three million square miles. About one-seventh of the world's land area is desert.

ARCTIC OCEAN

Russia

ASIA

Aral Sea

ROPE

China

K2

tican City

Caspian Sea

Kanchenjunga

Mount Everest

RICA

INDIAN OCEAN

AUSTRALASIA

ANTARCTICA

Q Where is the world's highest mountain?

A The world's highest mountain is Mount Everest. It lies in the Himalayas range in Central Asia and rises 29,028 feet above sea level. Some of the highest mountains in the world lie in this range. In the same range are K2 (28,250 feet) and Kanchenjunga (28,208 feet).

Q Where is the coldest place in the world?

A Antarctica is the coldest region in the world. It is the continent that surrounds the South Pole and is covered in a layer of ice about 1.5 miles thick. The temperature rarely rises above freezing point. In 1983, a temperature of -128.6 °F was recorded – the world's lowest ever.

OUR WORLD

COUNTRIES & PEOPLE

Q Which continent has most countries?

A The continent with the most countries is Africa. There are 53 independent countries in Africa. The largest African country is Sudan. It has an area of 966,757 square miles. The African country with the most people is Nigeria, with a population of over 92 million.

Mediterranean Sea

SUDAN

NIGERIA

Atlantic Ocean

Indian Ocean

Q Why do countries have flags?

A Every country has its own flag. Flags are used as a way of identifying the country, or anything belonging to it, to other nations. The flags above belong to countries that are members of the United Nations.

Q How many people are there in the world?

A More than 5.5 billion people live on the Earth. By the end of the 20th century the population will have reached 6.5 billion. Some places, such as deserts and polar regions, are largely unsuitable for people. Most people live where there is rich farmland or where cities can provide jobs and housing (below). The most populated country is China; it has over a billion people.

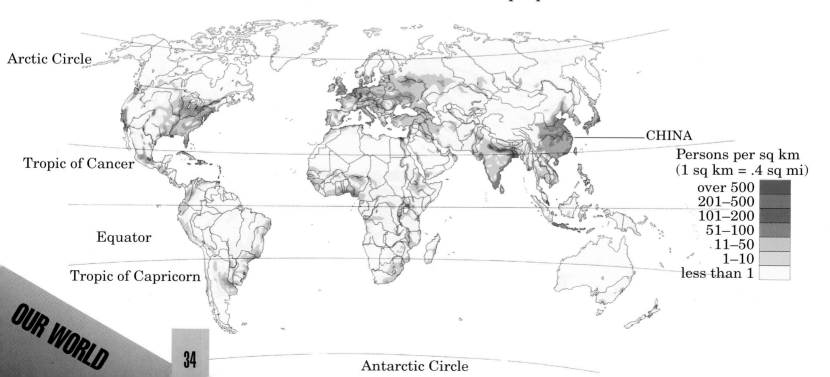

Arctic Circle

Tropic of Cancer

CHINA

Persons per sq km
(1 sq km = .4 sq mi)
over 500
201–500
101–200
51–100
11–50
1–10
less than 1

Equator

Tropic of Capricorn

Antarctic Circle

Q How many races of people are there?

A Over many thousands of years, people in different parts of the world have developed variations in appearance and hair or skin color. People of similar appearance and color are said to belong to the same race. Three of the main races are Negroid, Caucasoid, and Mongoloid (below). Their world distribution is shown on the map.

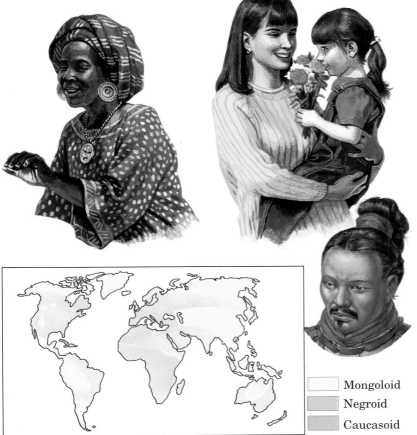

	Mongoloid
	Negroid
	Caucasoid

Q Why do people hold festivals?

A Festivals celebrate special days such as a time of year, like the Chinese New Year (below), or an important event such as the founding of a country, like Australia Day (right).

Q Why do people wear national costumes?

A Modern dress is similar in many parts of the world, so many people remember their heritage by wearing a national costume on festival days. The costume usually has a long history. The Breton people of northwest France have a very distinctive costume (right).

OUR WORLD

PEOPLE AT WORK

Q How does a diver breathe underwater?

A A diver uses scuba equipment to breathe underwater. Scuba stands for "self-contained underwater breathing apparatus." The diver (above) has metal tanks on his/her back that hold a mixture of oxygen and other gases so that the diver can breathe. The gases reach the diver's mouth through a hose.

Q What preflight checks must a pilot perform before takeoff?

A The pilot has to check both inside and outside the plane before he takes off. In the cockpit (above), he checks that there is enough fuel for the flight and that all the engine and flight controls are all working properly.

Q What do vets do?

A Vets only spend part of their time in their office (left). There, they treat family pets, such as rabbits, dogs, and cats. The rest of the time, vets travel to see bigger animals, especially on farms. They care for cows, pigs, sheep, and other livestock and help prevent outbreaks of animal diseases. Some vets inspect meat and eggs, or test milk and other animal products.

Q How does a farmer prepare soil for crops?

A First, the farmer plows the land (right). The sharp plowshares dig into the soil and turn it over. To break up the lumps of soil, the farmer pulls a sort of rake called a harrow, either with disks or with curved spikes, over the field. He may also crush the lumps with a heavy roller. At this stage, fertilizers are spread on the field to make the crops grow quickly. Then the field is ready for sowing.

Plowshare

Q Which fish are caught by deep-sea fishermen?

A Most fish are caught by modern fishing boats. Nearly 88 million tons of fish are caught every year. The main fish caught near the seabed are cod, flounder, hake, and pollack. These are often caught in funnel-shaped trawl nets. Fish enter through the net's wide mouth and collect at the narrow tail end. The fish must be preserved quickly or else they will spoil. Most deep-sea fishermen pack their catch in ice (below), or deep-freeze it, before sailing home.

Q How much equipment does a professional soccer player use?

A A professional soccer team has 20 to 30 fulltime players. Each player has at least five pairs of shoes, including training shoes and special shoes for use on hard ground. The team also uses nearly 1,000 pieces of clothing. These include game uniforms and tracksuits.

EVOLUTION

Q What is evolution?

A The first forms of life appeared on Earth many hundreds of millions of years ago. They were tiny, primitive creatures that lived in water. As millions of years went by, these creatures gradually changed and many different forms of life slowly appeared (above). This process is called evolution, and it is still continuing today.

Q How do we know about the past?

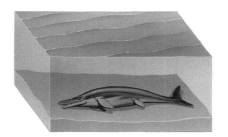

A We find out about the past from fossils. If a prehistoric animal died in shallow, muddy water, its body may have been covered with layers of silt which eventually formed solid rock. The soft parts decayed but the skeleton slowly absorbed minerals and hardened in the rock to become a fossil (left). Millions of years later, if the rock is worn away, we can find the fossil.

Q What does extinction mean?

A Extinction occurs when the last individual of a plant or animal species dies out. In the past, many creatures such as dinosaurs died out naturally – perhaps because of changes in the climate. In the last few centuries, animals such as the dodo (left) and the thylacine (below) have been hunted to extinction by people.

Q What is natural selection?

A Not all animals are as strong as others of the same species. This deer was not fast enough to escape a tiger attack, and it will be killed. Other, fitter deer will evade capture and survive to breed. This process of survival of the fittest is called natural selection.

Q How did the horse evolve?

A The horse evolved from a fox-sized forest animal called *Hyracotherium* that lived 50 million years ago. Its descendants, such as *Mesohippus* and *Merychippus,* grew larger and grazed on open grassland. The number of toes dwindled from four to one, and the animals ran on tiptoe. This improved their running speed. Eventually the modern horse evolved.

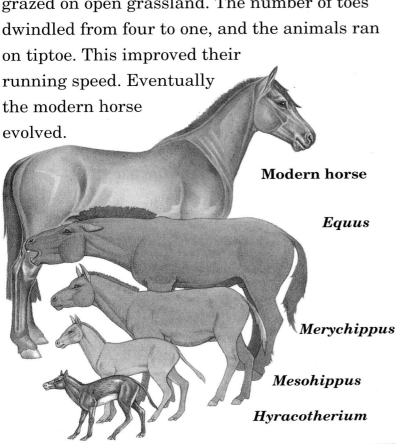

Modern horse

Equus

Merychippus

Mesohippus

Hyracotherium

Q What is adaptation?

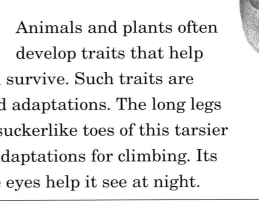

A Animals and plants often develop traits that help them survive. Such traits are called adaptations. The long legs and suckerlike toes of this tarsier are adaptations for climbing. Its large eyes help it see at night.

Q When did our ancestors evolve?

A Our line of evolution split off from apelike *Ramapithecus* about 12 million years ago. *Australopithecus* (right) was our first ancestor. It lived 5 million years ago. Then came *Homo habilis* 2 million years ago, then *Homo erectus* 1.6 million years ago. The first modern humans (*Homo sapiens*) appeared 400,000 years ago.

Q **Which animals were the first to fly?**

A Insects have been able to fly for far longer than any other animal. Winged insects probably developed from types of worms that lived in the sea. Some insects were huge, like the giant dragonfly *Meganeura* (right), which lived about 300 million years ago. Its wingspan was more than 24 inches.

PREHISTORIC LIFE

 Q **Why did animals begin to live on land?**

A The very earliest creatures lived in water. Then plants began to grow on the land. These provided a new source of food, and some animals left the water. They developed lungs, instead of gills, for breathing. Their fins developed into legs to help them move on land. The first to come on land were the amphibians such as *Ichthyostega*. They had fishlike heads and tails, but stronger backbones and stout legs.

Q **Which was the earliest known bird?**

A The *Archaeopteryx* (below) was a bird that lived about 150 million years ago. It looked like a small dinosaur but was covered with feathers. It also had wings which it spread for gliding through the air. Nobody knows for sure whether it could fly properly. Unlike today's birds, *Archaeopteryx* had three claws on each wing, which it used for climbing trees. It also had teeth and a long tail covered with feathers.

Q Why do dinosaurs have such long names?

A The names of dinosaurs look confusing, but they each describe something about their owner (right). The names are made up of Greek and Latin terms. The word dinosaur itself means "terrible lizard." *Corythosaurus* means "helmeted lizard." *Alamosaurus* means "lizard from Alamo." *Triceratops* means "face with three horns." *Tyrannosaurus* means "tyrant lizard." *Ornithomimus* means "imitator of birds." *Pachycephalosaurus* means "lizard with a thick head."

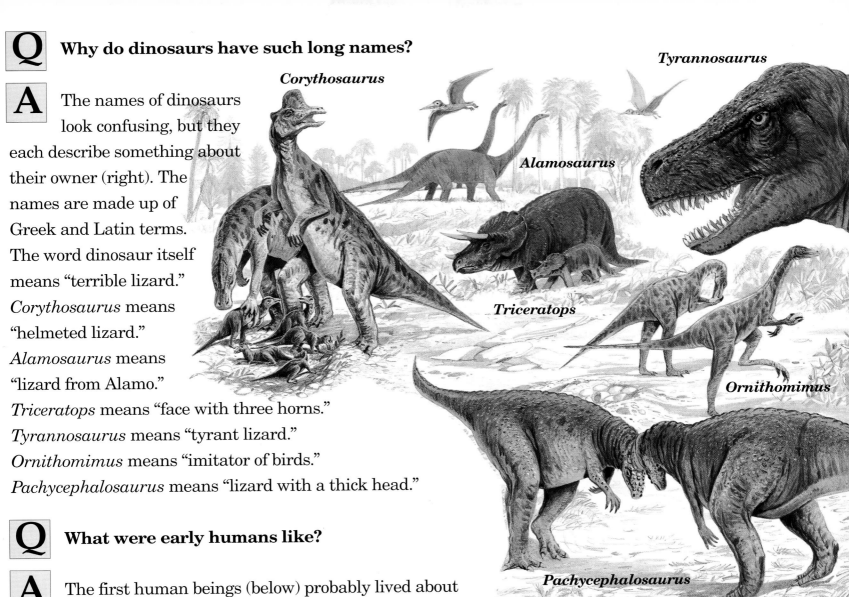

Corythosaurus

Tyrannosaurus

Alamosaurus

Triceratops

Ornithomimus

Pachycephalosaurus

Q What were early humans like?

A The first human beings (below) probably lived about 2 million years ago in East Africa. Their faces were apelike and their bodies were covered with hair. They walked upright and used sticks, stones, and bones as tools.

Q What is a fossil?

A A fossil is the remains of a plant or animal that lived millions of years ago. Some, like this insect (1), have been covered in a hard substance called amber. This is the sap from ancient pine trees. But most, like the plants (2, 3, and 5), have been turned into stone. The shell (4) is of an extinct marine animal called an ammonite.

1

2

3

4

5

NATURE

PREHISTORIC LIFE

Q What were the first animals like?

A The first animals were probably single-celled sea creatures. Their bodies had no hard parts, so they did not form fossils. The first animals that we know from fossils lived about 600 million years ago. Many had wormlike or plantlike bodies. Others had armored head shields (below).

Q How did *Pterodactylus* fly?

A *Pterodactylus* (above) had a lightweight body and was able to fly using its long, membranous wings. These were attached to the wrist bones and the bones of the fourth finger. *Pterodactylus* probably clung to cliff edges and then launched itself into the air, where it glided over the sea snatching fish from the surface.

Q What did prehistoric fish eat?

A Although no one can be completely sure, the diet of prehistoric fish probably consisted of wormlike creatures and mollusks. Some of the larger species of fish had numerous sharp teeth. They might have chased and eaten other fish, in a similar way to modern-day sharks and barracudas.

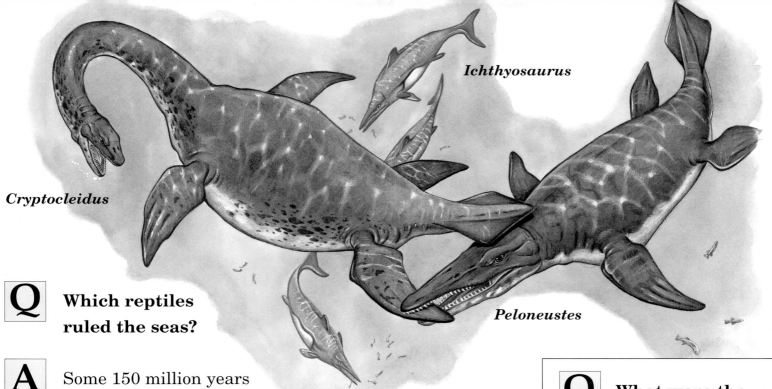

Cryptocleidus

Ichthyosaurus

Peloneustes

Q **Which reptiles ruled the seas?**

A Some 150 million years ago, the seas were ruled by ichthyosaurs and plesiosaurs (above). Both had streamlined bodies and paddle-shaped limbs. *Ichthyosaurus* resembled a cross between a fish and a dolphin. Some plesiosaurs, such as *Cryptocleidus,* had long necks; others, like *Peloneustes*, were whale-like. Ichthyosaurs and plesiosaurs ate mainly fish, but some plesiosaurs also ate one another.

Q **How did mammals survive the Ice Age?**

A As the Ice Age approached 1.6 million years ago, the climate became colder and many mammals grew larger. This is because large animals retain their body heat better than small ones. Heat retention was helped by growing thick, furry coats, such as that seen in the woolly mammoth (left). Thick layers of fat beneath the skin provided insulation. Other large, hairy mammals that survived the Ice Age included woolly rhinoceroses and giant cave bears.

Q **What were the terror cranes?**

A Terror cranes were giant birds that lived some 50 million years ago in North America. They stood 6½ feet tall and hunted small mammals in areas of open grassland. They had strong legs for running, and a powerful, hook-tipped bill for dealing with their prey. Terror cranes are given the scientific name *Diatryma.*

NATURE

DINOSAURS

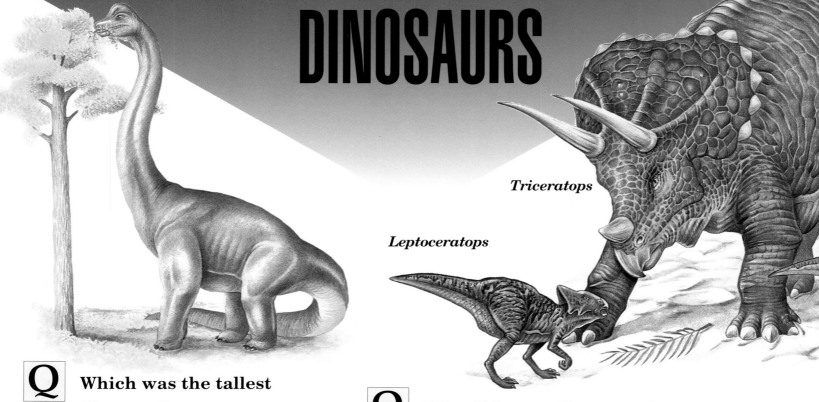

Triceratops

Leptoceratops

Q Which was the tallest dinosaur?

A Many of the huge, plant-eating dinosaurs had long necks. The tallest was *Brachiosaurus* (above), which not only had a long neck but also long front legs. It could stretch up to 40 feet and probably fed on the tops of trees, the way giraffes do today. It needed legs the size of tree trunks to support its great weight.

Q Why did some dinosaurs have armored heads?

A Some dinosaurs were meat-eating predators. Not surprisingly, many of the plant-eating dinosaurs developed armored heads to help defend themselves (above). The head of *Triceratops* was covered with a large plate and carried three forward-pointing horns. *Leptoceratops* was much smaller and lacked *Triceratops*' horns.

Q Which was the most fearsome meat eater?

A *Tyrannosaurus* (right) was probably the most terrifying carnivorous dinosaur. It was certainly one of the largest. The head was huge and its skull was larger than a person. *Tyrannosaurus* stood upright on massive hind legs and could outrun slower, plant-eating dinosaurs. Its teeth, which were six inches long, were used to rip and tear the flesh of its prey.

Tyrannosaurus **skull**

Q How did *Stegosaurus* get warm?

A *Stegosaurus* was a large, 25-foot-long dinosaur with a double row of armored plates on its back. These may have been useful in defense but were probably also used to control body temperature. They would have gathered heat from the Sun's rays to warm *Stegosaurus* up. Breezes passing through the plates would have helped *Stegosaurus* cool off if it was too hot.

Q Were all dinosaurs big?

A Although some dinosaurs were the largest land animals ever to have lived, many were tiny. Among the smallest were species of *Compsognathus* (left). Some were the size of a chicken. Most *Compsognathus* species had long legs and were good runners. This one is trying to catch a dragonfly.

Q How do we know what dinosaurs looked like?

A We can tell what dinosaurs looked like from fossils. These are found in sedimentary rocks from all over the world. Often just a few dinosaur bones are found, but sometimes scientists discover complete skeletons.

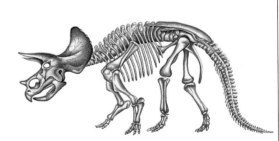

Q How does a jellyfish sting?

A A jellyfish (right) is a bell-shaped sea animal with its mouth underneath it. Its body is made of two layers of skin with a jellylike layer in between. Long tentacles hang down from the body. The tentacles have stinging cells which the jellyfish uses to stun its prey or protect itself from enemies. Humans can sometimes be hurt by these stings. Inside each stinging cell is a coiled thread (inset). When something touches the cell, the thread shoots out, sticking into the prey and injecting venom. In this way, jellyfish can catch large fish.

Q How many legs does a centipede have?

A A centipede's body is made up of segments. Each segment has one pair of legs attached to it. The centipede in this picture has 18 segments, so it has 36 legs. Some centipedes have only 15 segments and others have as many as 177 segments.

Q How does an octopus catch its food?

A An octopus (right) has eight tentacles and hunts on the seabed for fish or shellfish. It creeps toward its prey and then pounces, grabbing hold with its tentacles. Suckers on the tentacles hold the prey firmly while the octopus drags it to its mouth.

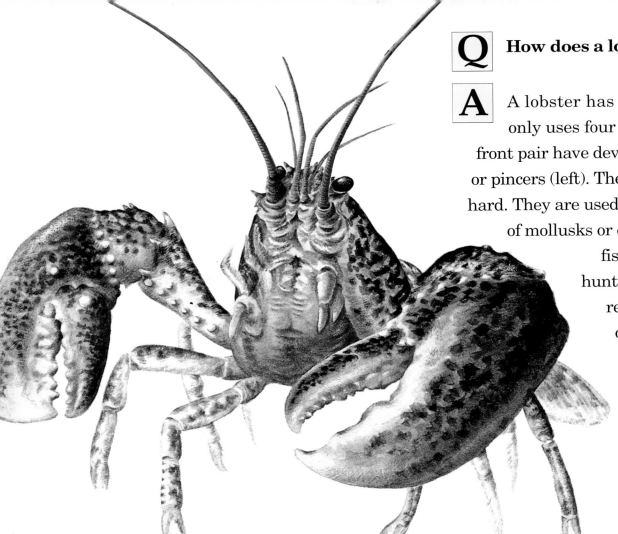

Q How does a lobster use its claws?

A A lobster has five pairs of legs, but only uses four pairs for walking. The front pair have developed into large claws or pincers (left). These are very strong and hard. They are used for crushing the shells of mollusks or even for catching small fish. But lobsters do little hunting and usually eat the remains of dead animals on the seabed. Lobsters also use their pincers to shred their food and to fight other lobsters.

Q How are hermit crabs different from other crabs?

A Hermit crabs have hard shells on their front parts, like other crabs, but their abdomens are soft. They live inside the empty shells of other sea animals for protection.

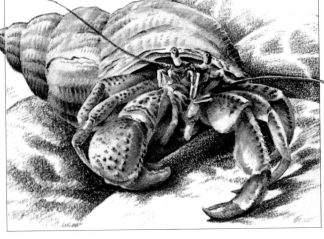

Q Is a starfish really a fish?

A Starfish (below) are not fish – they belong to the group of sea animals called echinoderms. The name means "spiny-skinned." Starfish have arms, but no head, and no front or back. They move slowly by gripping the seabed with water-filled tubes on their arms. The starfish's arms are so strong that they can pull apart the two shells of a mussel to reach the food inside.

NATURE

SIMPLE CREATURES

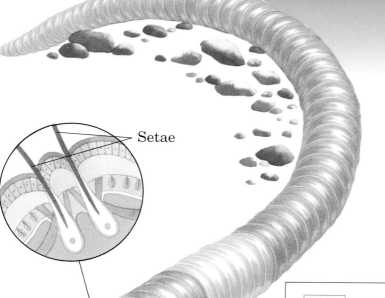

Setae

Segments

Mouth

Q What is inside an earthworm?

A An earthworm's body (left) is made up of compartments called segments. The intestine and the nervous system run the entire length of the body. The hearts, brain, and reproductive organs are found near the front of the body. Each segment carries bristly hairs called setae. These help the worm grip the ground when moving.

Q Are sea anemones plants or animals?

A Sea anemones are marine animals. They live attached to rocks, and have a ring of stinging tentacles around their mouth which they use for catching food. Some sea anemones can pull the tentacles inside (right).

Q What is a protozoan?

A Protozoans are tiny animals that consist of a single cell. Although small, these cells are very complex and enable the animal to eat, breathe, excrete, and reproduce. Protozoans are very common in soil and water. Some have a rigid shape, while others have no fixed shape at all.

Actinosphaerium

Difflugia

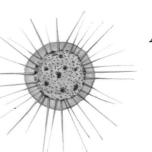

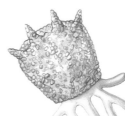

Amoeba

Q How does a Portuguese man-of-war swim?

A The Portuguese man-of-war (left) is a large, poisonous, jellyfish-like creature with tentacles up to 60 feet long. It lives in the ocean but does not actually swim. It has a float filled with air that keeps it on the surface, and a sail that carries the animal on the breeze.

Q Why do crabs walk sideways?

A Crabs have their walking legs placed beneath their bodies. If it were to walk forward or backward, the crab would trip over its own legs. Instead, crabs scuttle sideways over the seabed so their legs do not touch.

Q How does the cleaner shrimp get its name?

A The cleaner shrimp (below) removes parasites from fish such as this butterfly fish. Both animals benefit. The shrimp gets a tasty meal, and the fish loses a parasite that it would be unable to dislodge on its own.

Q What animal is destroying the Great Barrier Reef?

A The crown-of-thorns starfish (below) lives in tropical seas. It is common on the Great Barrier Reef off the coast of Australia. It turns its stomach inside out to eat the soft-bodied coral animals. Its skin is armored with fearsome spines, and it has few predators. The crown-of-thorns has destroyed large areas of coral reef.

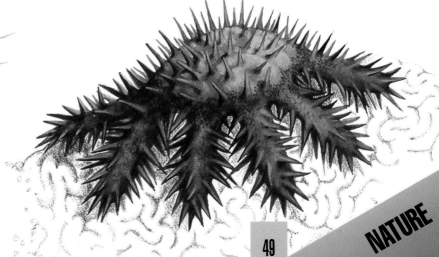

NATURE

INSECTS & SPIDERS

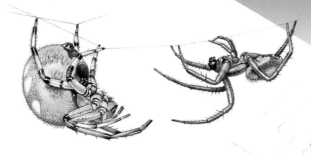

Q How does a spider make a web?

A Spiders make silk in glands near their abdomens. They draw the silk out into threads to build insect traps called webs. The orb spider (right) first fixes threads in a box shape. Then it weaves more threads to the center. The threads are covered in sticky droplets to catch insects.

Q What is a stick insect?

A Stick insects (right) have long thin bodies with brown or green coloring that makes them look just like the twigs or leaves they sit on. Their enemies, such as birds or lizards, often fail to see them. If they are attacked, stick insects fall to the ground and lie still, once again becoming difficult to see.

Q What is inside an insect?

A An insect's body (right) has many of the organs we have, such as a brain and a heart, but they work differently. Insects breathe through holes called spiracles in their hard outer covering. Their gut is a tube running from the mouth to the end of the abdomen. Their blood runs in an open system throughout the body. All the organs are bathed in blood.

Brain

Heart

Foregut

Midgut

Compound eye

Hindgut

Spiracles

Abdomen

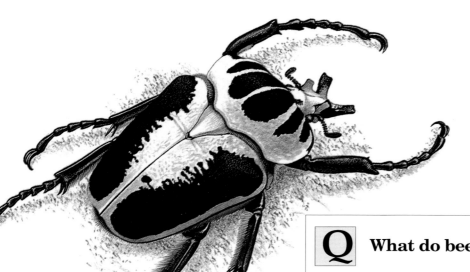

Q Which insect is the heaviest?

A The African Goliath beetle (left) is the heaviest of all insects. It grows to almost 5 inches and weighs up to 4 ounces. The lightest insect is the parasitic wasp called the fairy fly, which is less than 0.2 mm long and weighs just 0.006 grams.

Q What do bees and wasps eat?

A Bees eat pollen and nectar, which they collect from plants, store in their nests, and turn into honey. Wasps kill other insects as food for their young, or larvae.

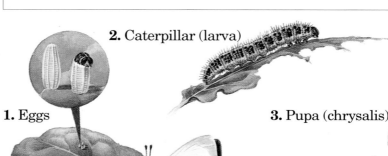

Bee   Wasp

Q How do grasshoppers "sing"?

A Grasshoppers make sounds by rubbing small pegs on their hind legs against a hard vein on their forewings. Males "sing" to attract a mate.

2. Caterpillar (larva)

1. Eggs

3. Pupa (chrysalis)

Q How does a butterfly begin its life?

A A butterfly begins life as an egg on a leaf. Out of the egg comes a tiny caterpillar (or larva), which eats the leaf and grows very fast. The caterpillar grows a hard covering and turns into a pupa (or chrysalis). After several days, or even weeks, the pupa case splits open and the butterfly crawls out. As soon as its wings have dried, it can fly away (right).

4. Adult butterflies

NATURE

INSECTS & SPIDERS

Q How does
the praying mantis get its name?

A The praying mantis (below)
is a fierce, predatory insect that
catches other insects for food. Its front pair of
legs are specially adapted for grabbing prey. As
the mantis is stalking its victim, these legs
are held folded under its head.
When it does this, it looks as
if it might be praying, and
this is how it got its
name.

Q Which
spider is the
most poisonous?

A Although fairly small, the black
widow (above) may be the most
deadly spider. There are several
different species which live in warm
areas such as North America and
Australia. Because it likes dark, shady
places, the spider often goes into
houses. It is therefore more likely
to bite people than other
poisonous spiders.

Q How do ants live?

A Ants are insects that live in colonies.
Their large underground nests (right)
contain thousands of individual ants, and have a
series of chambers and tunnels. One important
chamber will be home to the queen ant. She lays
thousands of eggs which soon hatch into ant
larvae. These are fed by the worker
ants. Then they turn into pupae
from which adult ants
finally emerge.

Queen ant

Eggs

Worker an
keep green
and "milk"
them for
honeyde

Worker ant

Larvae

Adult ants breal
out of pupae

Worker ant bringing food

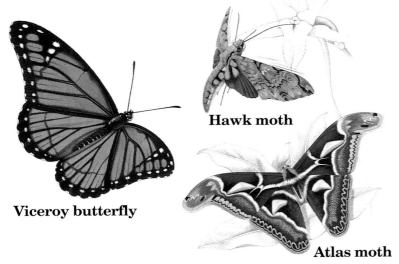

Hawk moth

Viceroy butterfly

Atlas moth

Q **Do insects have territories?**

A A few insects do have territories which they defend against others of their kind. These two male stalk-eyed flies (right) from Africa are assessing each other's size by measuring their eye stalks. The prize for the winner is to mate with any female that enters the territory.

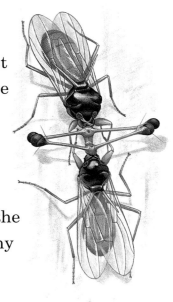

Q **How can you tell butterflies and moths apart?**

A Although similar insects to look at, butterflies fly by day while moths mostly fly at night. Most butterflies have club-tipped antennae while moths usually have straight or feathery antennae (above). Butterflies usually close their wings together at rest.

Q **How many different kinds of insects are there?**

A Nobody knows for sure how many different insects there are. It has been estimated, however, that there may be more than 30 million kinds, or species, in a huge variety of shapes and sizes. Examples from the major groups, or orders, of insects are shown below.

Q **Why are some insects brightly colored?**

A Some insects have bright colors to attract one another to mate. Others, such as this ladybug, advertise the fact that they taste nasty by being colorful. Birds and other predators soon learn to associate bright colors and bold patterns with creatures that taste nasty or that might be poisonous.

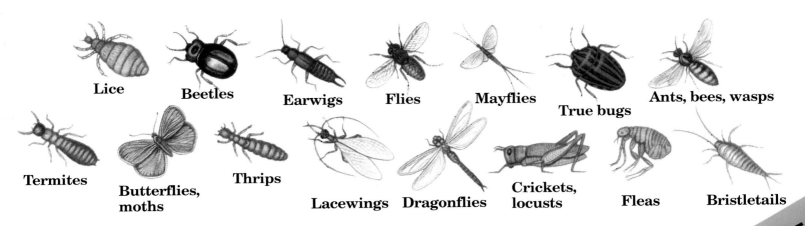

Lice   **Beetles**   **Earwigs**   **Flies**   **Mayflies**   **True bugs**   **Ants, bees, wasps**

Termites   **Butterflies, moths**   **Thrips**   **Lacewings**   **Dragonflies**   **Crickets, locusts**   **Fleas**   **Bristletails**

FISH

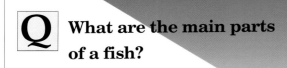

Q What are the main parts
of a fish?

A The main parts on the outside of a fish are the gills
(for breathing), the fins (for swimming and steering),
and the lateral line (for detecting movement nearby).

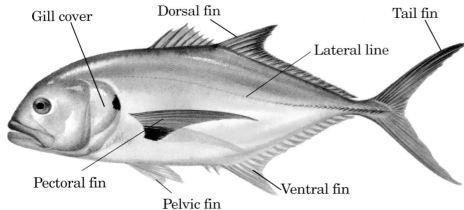

Gill cover

Dorsal fin

Tail fin

Lateral line

Pectoral fin

Ventral fin

Pelvic fin

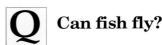

Q Can fish fly?

A Flying fish (above) have large
pectoral fins which act as wing
Their tails propel them out of the
water to glide at speeds of 40 mph.

Basking shark

Dogfish

Skate

Q How many kinds of shark are there?

A The shark family contains about 340 species
of all shapes and sizes. One of the biggest is
the basking shark (above), which feeds on plankton
and tiny fish. Dogfish and skates live on the
ocean floor. Saw sharks have long snouts
with sharp, sawlike teeth.

Saw shark

NATURE

54

Q Which fish swims the fastest?

A Sailfish are the fastest swimmers, reaching speeds of up to 68 mph. The fish's large dorsal fin can lie flat against its body to help streamline it when it is swimming at high speed.

Loosejaw

Viperfish

Anglerfish

Hatchetfish

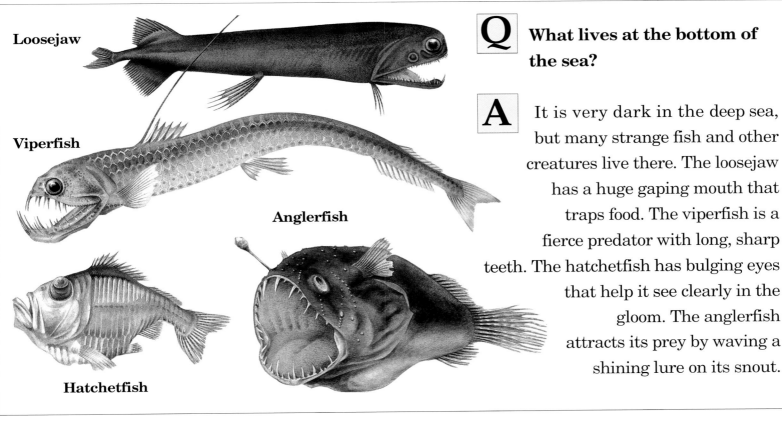

Q What lives at the bottom of the sea?

A It is very dark in the deep sea, but many strange fish and other creatures live there. The loosejaw has a huge gaping mouth that traps food. The viperfish is a fierce predator with long, sharp teeth. The hatchetfish has bulging eyes that help it see clearly in the gloom. The anglerfish attracts its prey by waving a shining lure on its snout.

Q Do all fish lay eggs?

A No. Several species, such as the sailfin molly (below), keep their eggs inside until they hatch. Then they give birth to as many as 200 live young.

Q How do cod find their food?

A Some species of fish, such as the Atlantic cod (below) have a single whiskerlike projection on their chin to help them feel for their food. This is called a barbel.

NATURE

FISH

Q Which fish climbs trees?

A The mudskipper (below) lives in African mangrove swamps. Because it can take in oxygen through its mouth and throat, it can venture onto the mud flats when the tide is out. If danger threatens and it cannot get back to its burrow, it can climb mangrove roots to escape.

Q What is unusual about the seahorse?

A Apart from its curious shape, the seahorse (right) is unusual because it is the male and not the female who looks after the eggs and young. He has a brood pouch on his belly, and this can hold up to 200 eggs and young. When the young are old enough, the male expels them from the pouch.

Q How does a fish sense its surroundings?

A Although most fish have good eyesight and a sense of taste, they also use a structure called the lateral line (right). This groove lies along the side of a fish's body, and contains special cells that are sensitive to vibrations in the water. With this, the fish can detect both food and danger.

Lateral line

Q How does a shark hunt its prey?

A Although sharks have poor eyesight, they have an excellent sense of smell. They can detect blood diluted a million times in water and will home in on a wounded animal in the sea. Sharks are also able to detect vibrations in the water caused, for example, by the thrashing movements of an injured fish.

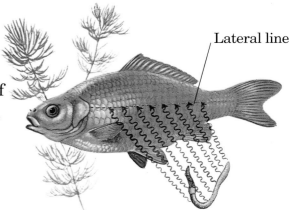

Q Which fish
can spear boats?

A Although they do not do it often,
swordfish (right) have been known to
spear the hulls of wooden boats. They have a
snout that is long and pointed. The swordfish
probably uses this to slash at prey and predators. It is
one of the fastest fish, swimming at up to 62 miles per hour.

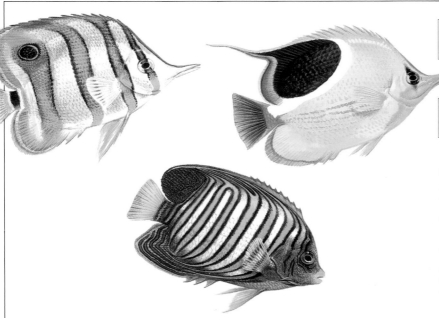

Q How do butterfly fish get their
name?

A Butterfly fish get their name
because they are very brightly
colored, like the wings of a butterfly.
Most species are found on coral reefs in
tropical waters around the world. The
colors and patterns are thought to confuse
predators. They may also help the fish
blend into its surroundings to hide.

Q How does a flounder avoid its
enemies?

A The flounder (below) is a flatfish
that lives on the sandy seabed. Its
markings and colors help it blend in
with its surroundings, for camouflage.
The flounder can also flick
sand over its body using
its fins.
Often only
the head
and eyes
remain visible.

NATURE

AMPHIBIANS & REPTILES

Q Where do cobras live?

A The Indian cobra lives in southern Asia. When threatened, it spreads the ribs in its neck, forming a hood. This makes it appear bigger and frightens its enemy. The ringhals is an African cobra. The coral snake, which belongs to the cobra family, lives in American forests.

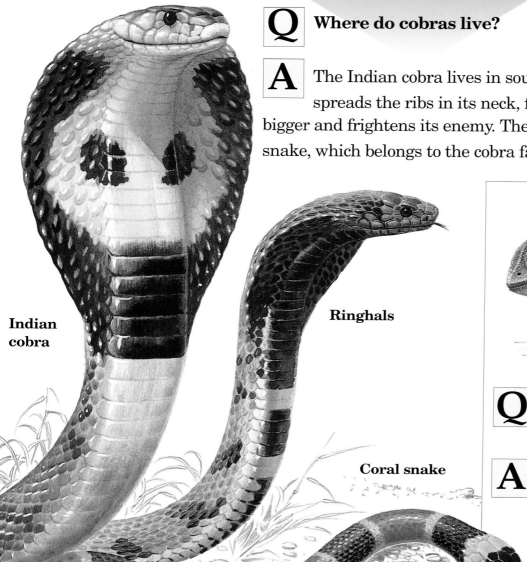

Indian cobra

Ringhals

Coral snake

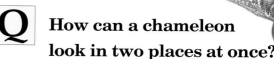

Q How can a chameleon look in two places at once?

A A chameleon can swivel its eyes separately. One may be looking forward, and the other backward. The eyes can also work together to focus on the same object.

Alligator

Crocodile

Q How can you tell the difference between an alligator and a crocodile?

A When a crocodile closes its mouth, the fourth tooth in the lower jaw sticks up outside the top jaw. When an alligator does the same thing, this tooth is hidden.

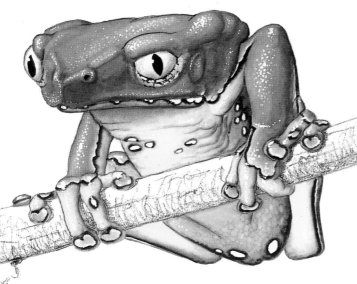

Q How do frogs climb trees?

A The tree frog (left) has round disks at the end of its toes. These act as suckers and help the frog climb up smooth leaves. The toes are long and can curl around thin twigs. Some tree frogs have sticky webbing between their fingers and toes that enables them to hold on more easily. The frog's belly skin is loose, and this also clings to the tree.

Q Why do reptiles flick out their tongues?

A This monitor lizard (right) is flicking out its tongue. Sometimes the tongue touches the ground, and sometimes it waves in the air. The tongue collects tiny chemical traces and takes them back to the mouth, where nerve cells figure out what the chemicals mean. By doing this, the monitor can pick up signals about food dangers nearby. Many lizards and snakes use their tongues in the same way.

Q How do frogs jump?

A A frog hops and leaps in just the same way as it swims. It lifts its front legs off the ground and pushes off with its powerful back legs (left). The pressure forces open the large webbed feet, giving the frog a firm base from which to jump. It lands on its front legs and chest and then gathers in its back legs, ready for another leap.

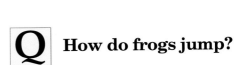

AMPHIBIANS & REPTILES

Q Are all snakes poisonous?

A Many snakes are perfectly harmless to humans and do not have poison fangs or venom. Although it may look menacing, this Arafura wart snake (above), which lives in rivers in Australia and New Guinea, does not have a poisonous bite.

Q What is a salamander?

A Salamanders such as this tiger salamander (right) are related to newts, and both are amphibians. Salamanders are perfectly at home on land but have to live in damp places. This is because their skins lose water easily. Some species can breed on land, but many return to water to spawn. Salamanders eat small creatures such as worms and slugs.

Q How do frogs breathe?

A Like other amphibians, frogs have lungs that they use to take in air and absorb oxygen into their blood. They are also able to take up oxygen through their skins. In order to do this, however, they have to keep their bodies moist at all times. Frogs are also able to absorb oxygen through the moist lining of their mouth.

Q Which turtle travels farthest?

A Most turtles travel long distances during their lives. The green turtle (left), however, probably holds the record. Individuals that feed off the coast of South America travel 1,367 miles to Ascension Island to breed. Turtles make these long-distance journeys because the number of beaches suitable for egg-laying is small.

Q How does the collared lizard escape?

A The collared lizard (right) lives on grassy plains in North America. In order to escape from danger, the lizard is able to run on its back legs. It is able, therefore, to move at faster speeds than if it had to scurry on all four legs.

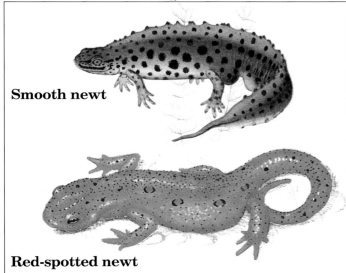

Smooth newt

Red-spotted newt

Q How do newts find their way home?

A Newts such as the smooth newt and the red-spotted newt spend much of their lives on land but return to water to breed. They often find the pond where they themselves were spawned. Most species use taste and smell to help them navigate. A few species also use the Sun or the Earth's magnetism to check the direction they are traveling in.

Q Which reptiles can change color?

A Chameleons (left) are able to change their color to match their background. They do this by moving pigment around in their skin, and the change can be complete in just a few minutes. Chameleons use this ability to change color for camouflage. This way they can avoid being spotted by predators. They can also get closer to prey without being seen.

BIRDS

Q Which bird sleeps in the air?

A The swift (below) sleeps, eats, and even mates in the air. It is perfectly built for flying. Its long, swept-back wings help it fly fast and high in the sky, where it hunts for insects. But its legs and feet are weak. It is hard for swifts to hop or walk. Some swifts spend almost all their lives flying.

Q How can owls hunt in the dark?

A The owl (below) listens for the sounds of shrews or mice. It swivels its head until the sound is equally loud in both ears. The owl can then pinpoint exactly where the sound is coming from.

Q How do penguins keep their eggs warm?

A King penguins (right) live near the cold South Pole. The females each lay one egg on the ice in midwinter. The male penguin tucks the egg between his feet and his bulging stomach to keep it warm, until it hatches about two months later.

Q Why do parrots "talk"?

A In the wild, parrots are sociable birds and call to each other with clicks, squeaks, and screams. When they are kept in captivity they sometimes seem to speak like humans. However, the parrots are not really speaking. They are just copying human voices.

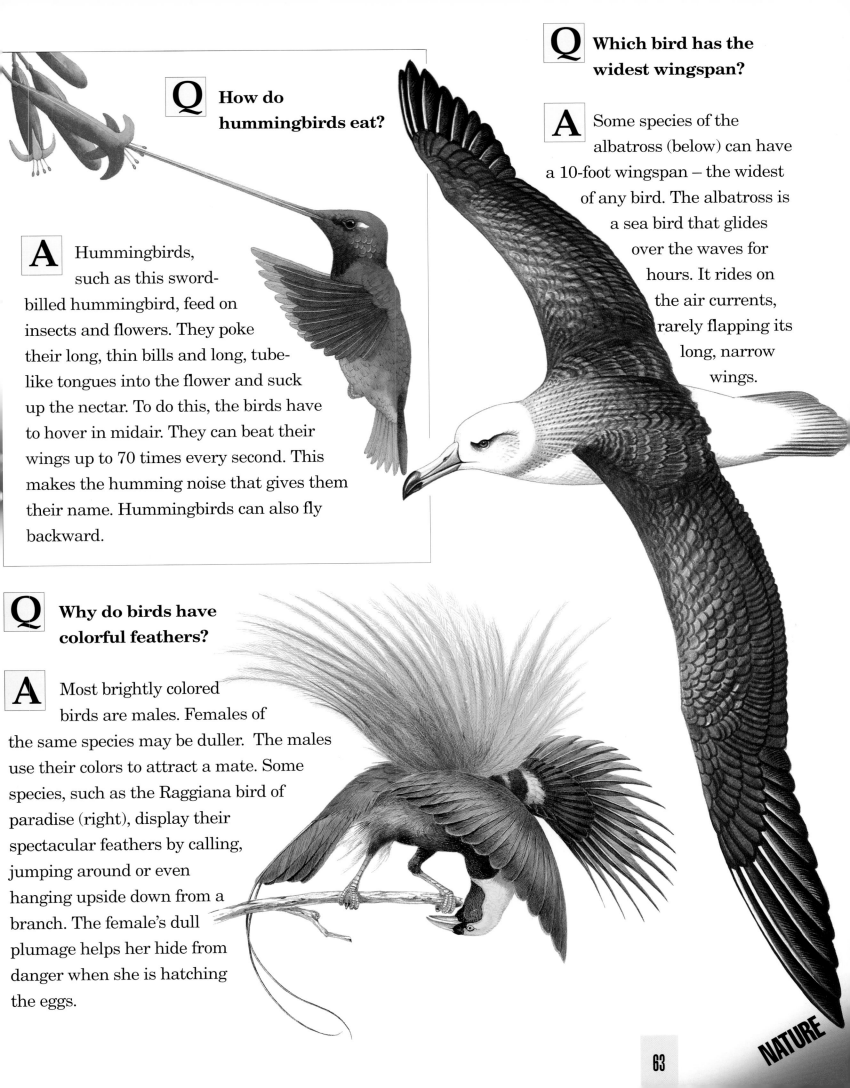

Q **How do hummingbirds eat?**

A Hummingbirds, such as this sword-billed hummingbird, feed on insects and flowers. They poke their long, thin bills and long, tube-like tongues into the flower and suck up the nectar. To do this, the birds have to hover in midair. They can beat their wings up to 70 times every second. This makes the humming noise that gives them their name. Hummingbirds can also fly backward.

Q **Which bird has the widest wingspan?**

A Some species of the albatross (below) can have a 10-foot wingspan – the widest of any bird. The albatross is a sea bird that glides over the waves for hours. It rides on the air currents, rarely flapping its long, narrow wings.

Q **Why do birds have colorful feathers?**

A Most brightly colored birds are males. Females of the same species may be duller. The males use their colors to attract a mate. Some species, such as the Raggiana bird of paradise (right), display their spectacular feathers by calling, jumping around or even hanging upside down from a branch. The female's dull plumage helps her hide from danger when she is hatching the eggs.

NATURE

BIRDS

Q Why are birds' beaks different?

A Each bird species has a beak whose shape is best suited to the way it feeds. Birds of prey (1) have hooked beaks for tearing flesh, while waders (2) have long beaks for probing the mud for worms. Kookaburras (3) have stabbing beaks for catching reptiles, while nightjars (4) have wide gapes to catch flying insects. Puffins (5) use their beaks both for catching food and to send signals.

Q Why do vultures have bald heads?

A Vultures (right) feed on the carcasses of dead animals. They sometimes have to push their heads inside the body in order to get a meal. If they had feathers on their heads and necks, these would soon become clogged and matted with blood.

Q Which bird is the pirate of the air?

A Frigate birds are large sea birds that live in the tropics. Instead of catching their own food, they behave like pirates toward other birds. When a frigate bird sees a bird such as a booby returning from a fishing trip, it chases it. It pulls the victim's tail and wings until it drops its food. The frigate bird then catches the fish in midair.

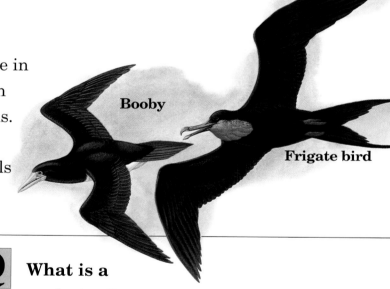

Booby

Frigate bird

Q What is a cockatoo?

A Cockatoos are types of parrot. They can raise their head feathers to form a crest. Most species come from Australia and New Guinea. The palm cockatoo is the largest cockatoo and also the largest Australian parrot. It lives in rain forests. The galah is sometimes called the roseate cockatoo and also comes from Australia. It is the commonest cockatoo and lives near farmland.

Galah

Palm cockatoo

Q How many feathers does a bird have?

A The number of feathers on a bird varies according to the species, its age, and the season. Most small songbirds have between 1,500 and 3,000 feathers on their bodies. A swan, however, might have as many as 25,000 feathers. A bird of prey, such as this eagle (left), would have between 5,000 and 8,000 feathers.

Q How does a woodpecker find its food?

A Woodpeckers (below) have large, chisel-like bills and a strong skull. When they tap the trunk of a tree, they can tell if an insect grub is living inside by the sound the tapping makes. When they find a likely spot, they smash open the wood with heavy blows of their bill. They can then take the insect to eat.

Q How did the secretary bird get its name?

A Secretary birds (right) have strange-looking feathers arranged on their heads. When the first explorers visited Africa and saw these birds they reminded them of Victorian secretaries who used to keep their quill pens behind their ears. Secretary birds catch snakes with their long legs.

NATURE

SEA MAMMALS

Q What is the largest animal in the world?

A The blue whale (below) is the largest animal that has ever lived on this planet. It can grow to 90 feet long, and weigh 200 tons.

Q Can polar bears swim?

A Polar bears (above) are strong swimmers, and can travel long distances in the icy waters of the Arctic. Their fur is thick and waterproof, and their feet are partly webbed.

Q Which whale can dive the deepest?

A The sperm whale (right) can dive to a depth of more than 10,000 feet. It goes down to the seabed in search of squid to eat. Sperm whales can spend over an hour under water before coming to the surface to breathe.

Q What is a dugong?

A A dugong, or sea cow, is a mammal that lives in the warm waters of the southwest Pacific. It eats sea grasses, which it digs up from the shallows. It is a good swimmer, with a flat, forked tail.

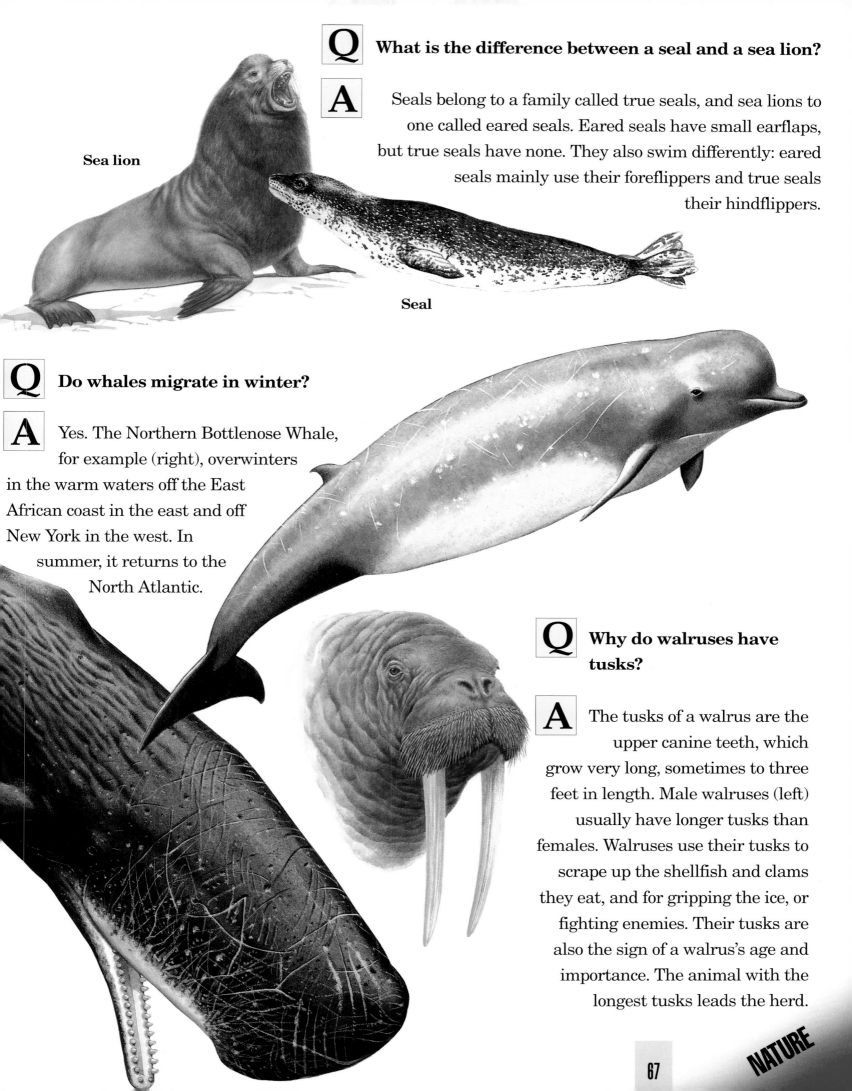

Q What is the difference between a seal and a sea lion?

A Seals belong to a family called true seals, and sea lions to one called eared seals. Eared seals have small earflaps, but true seals have none. They also swim differently: eared seals mainly use their foreflippers and true seals their hindflippers.

Sea lion

Seal

Q Do whales migrate in winter?

A Yes. The Northern Bottlenose Whale, for example (right), overwinters in the warm waters off the East African coast in the east and off New York in the west. In summer, it returns to the North Atlantic.

Q Why do walruses have tusks?

A The tusks of a walrus are the upper canine teeth, which grow very long, sometimes to three feet in length. Male walruses (left) usually have longer tusks than females. Walruses use their tusks to scrape up the shellfish and clams they eat, and for gripping the ice, or fighting enemies. Their tusks are also the sign of a walrus's age and importance. The animal with the longest tusks leads the herd.

NATURE

SEA MAMMALS

Bottle-nosed dolphin

Common porpoise

Q **What is the difference between a dolphin and a porpoise?**

A Most dolphins have a beaklike nose and a large swelling on the forehead. Porpoises, which are the smallest of the whales, have a somewhat stubby head and never have a beak. Dolphins and porpoises are both types of small whale. They feed on fish and can swim very fast to catch their prey.

Q **Which animal is called the sea canary?**

A The beluga whale (above), which lives in Arctic seas, is called the sea canary. This is because it makes a wide variety of whistling and chirping noises. In the summer, belugas move into the mouths of rivers to feed on migrating salmon. They sometimes gather in large numbers to feed, and their canary-like sounds can be heard from above the water as well as from below. Adult belugas are white, but their young are darker in color.

Q **How did the right whale get its name?**

A Sad though it may seem, early whalers gave the right whale its name. They considered it to be the "right" whale to catch because it was a slow swimmer and floated after it had been killed. Some species of whale sink after they have been killed and would have been difficult for early whalers to tow back to their ship. Right whales were nearly hunted to extinction.

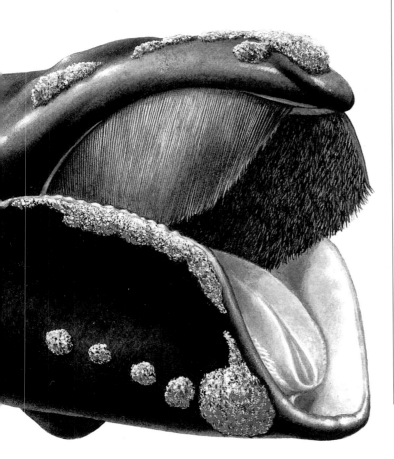

 Which is the most ferocious sea mammal?

 The killer whale (below) is the most ferocious sea mammal. It eats fish, squid, sharks, and even seals, porpoises, and walruses. Sometimes killer whales launch themselves from the sea to snatch seals from the beach. Packs of killer whales have even been known to attack animals as large as blue whales. Surprisingly, attacks on humans have never been known, and killer whales can be watched closely from boats.

 How does the sea otter eat clams?

A The sea otter lives in the Pacific waters off northern California. It has developed a clever method of opening clams and mussel shells to reach the food inside. Lying on its back on the surface of the sea, the sea otter places a large stone on its chest. It then strikes the clam or mussel shell against the stone until the shell shatters. The sea otter then eats the flesh inside the shell.

LAND MAMMALS

Q How do bats locate their food?

A Bats (left) have weak eyes, so they use their ears to locate flying insects. They send out high-pitched noises and listen for the echoes. They can tell if the echo comes from an insect, and figure out exactly where it is.

Q What is the smallest land mammal?

A The pygmy white-toothed shrew (above) is the smallest mammal that lives on land. It measures only 1½ inches and weighs about ⅒ ounce. Pygmy shrews live in Africa, and eat spiders, grasshoppers, and cockroaches – which may be almost as big as they are.

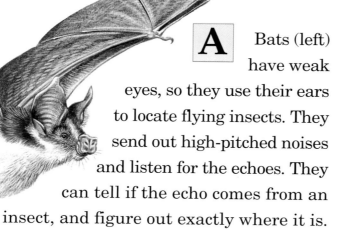

African elephant   Asian elephant

Q What is the difference between the African and Asian elephant?

A The African elephant is bigger than the Asian, and has larger ears. It also has two lips at the tip of its trunk instead of one.

Q Which is the fastest mammal?

A The cheetah (right) can sprint in short bursts at a speed of nearly 62 mph, faster than any other land animal. It stalks its prey until it is very close, then breaks cover and runs in long, fast strides.

Q How does a camel survive in the desert?

A Camels (right) can go for weeks without drinking. They lose very little water from their sweat or urine. The camel's fur coat protects it from the heat of the Sun, and it can close its nostrils to keep out sand and dust. Wide feet help it walk over soft sand without sinking. Despite popular belief, camels do not store water in their humps. The humps are used to store fat, which is used for food.

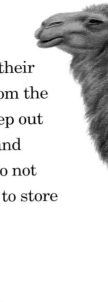

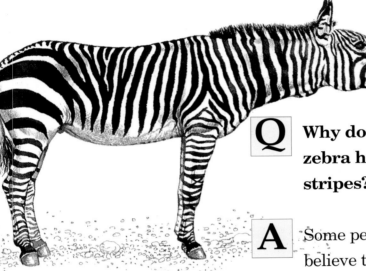

Q Why does a zebra have stripes?

A Some people believe that a zebra's stripes (above) act as a sort of camouflage, making individual animals hard to spot. But now scientists think there are other reasons for the stripes. They may dazzle lions and other cats that attack the zebra. Or they may help the members of a zebra herd recognize each other.

Q How can you tell a monkey from an ape?

A Monkeys and apes are both primates. Apes, such as the gorilla, have no tails. They have strong arms which are longer than their legs. Most monkeys, like the woolly monkey, have tails with which they can hang from trees.

Woolly Monkey

Gorilla

NATURE

LAND MAMMALS

Q Which animal is called the "walking pine cone"?

A This name is used to describe the pangolin (left). It is also sometimes called the scaly anteater. Most of the pangolin's body is covered in hard, protective, overlapping scales. When threatened, it curls into a ball. Some pangolins can climb trees.

Q Which animal is called the river horse?

A The hippopotamus (above) is sometimes called the river horse. In fact its name is made up of Greek words meaning "river" and "horse." Hippos live in Africa and spend much of the day partly under the water in rivers and lakes. After dark, they may come out to feed on the plants on the bank. Hippos can be quarrelsome animals, and two males will often fight one another, sometimes causing severe injuries.

Q What is a rhino's horn made of?

A Although it may look solid and bony, the horn of a rhino (below) is made of the same material as hair and hooves. Rhinos are sometimes illegally killed for their horns, in the belief that the horn makes a good medicine. As a result, rhinos are rare and endangered today even though the trade in their horns is banned in most countries.

Q How does a mongoose defeat a cobra?

A The deadly cobra is usually no match for a mongoose. The mongoose is extremely agile, and leaps away when the snake tries to strike. Soon the snake tires, and then the mongoose attacks, killing the snake with a bite to the neck.

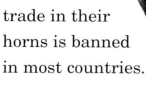

Q How does a lion catch its prey?

A Although its prey may be fast-moving, a lion is stealthy and will creep close to its victim before making its attack. Lions often work as a team with different individuals cutting off the prey's line of escape. Animals such as this wildebeest (right) are sometimes killed with a bite to the neck that crushes the vertebrae. On other occasions, the lion suffocates its prey by gripping on to the throat.

Q How do kangaroos and wallabies run?

A Kangaroos and wallabies run using their large and powerful back legs to hop. The small front legs are used only for feeding and grooming. The long, robust tail helps the animal balance when it is hopping. Some kangaroos can reach speeds of 25 mph or more and are able to hop for long periods of time. Kangaroos live in Australia.

Q How does the porcupine protect itself?

A The sharp, spiny quills of a porcupine are really just specially strengthened hairs. In some species, such as the African porcupine (left), they can reach a length of 20 inches. The quills are so strong that they can cause painful injuries if they are jabbed into a would-be attacker.

ECOLOGY

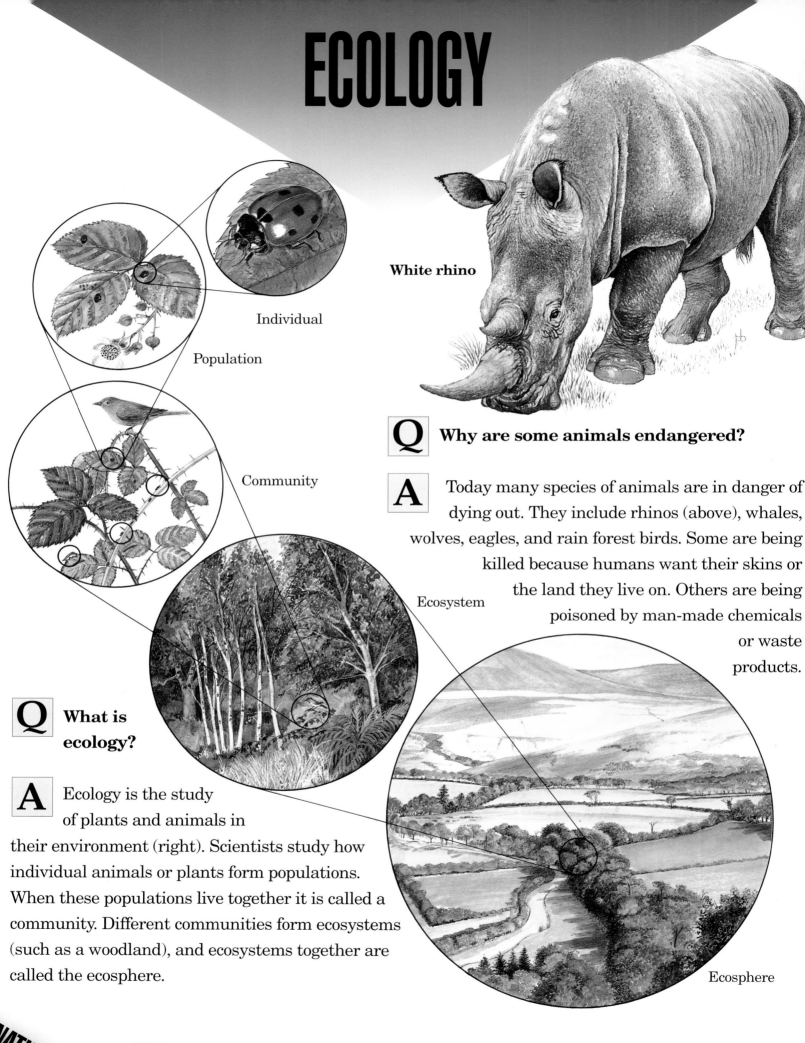

Individual

Population

Community

Ecosystem

Ecosphere

White rhino

Q Why are some animals endangered?

A Today many species of animals are in danger of dying out. They include rhinos (above), whales, wolves, eagles, and rain forest birds. Some are being killed because humans want their skins or the land they live on. Others are being poisoned by man-made chemicals or waste products.

Q What is ecology?

A Ecology is the study of plants and animals in their environment (right). Scientists study how individual animals or plants form populations. When these populations live together it is called a community. Different communities form ecosystems (such as a woodland), and ecosystems together are called the ecosphere.

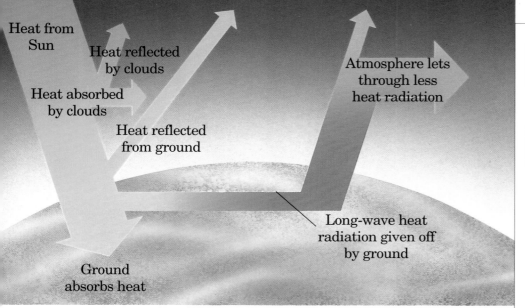

Heat from Sun

Heat reflected by clouds

Heat absorbed by clouds

Heat reflected from ground

Atmosphere lets through less heat radiation

Long-wave heat radiation given off by ground

Ground absorbs heat

Q What is the greenhouse effect?

A Heat comes to the Earth from the Sun. Most of it is then reflected back into space. But some gases trap the heat inside the Earth's atmosphere, which grows very hot like a greenhouse. This is what is known as the greenhouse effect (above).

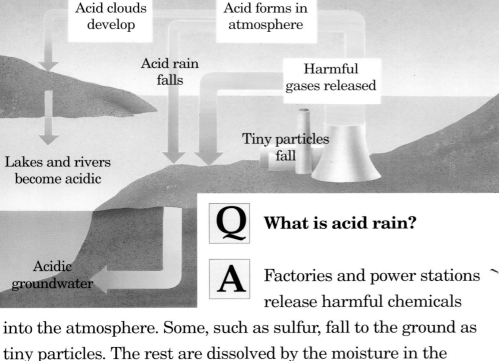

Acid clouds develop

Acid forms in atmosphere

Acid rain falls

Harmful gases released

Tiny particles fall

Lakes and rivers become acidic

Acidic groundwater

Q What is acid rain?

A Factories and power stations release harmful chemicals into the atmosphere. Some, such as sulfur, fall to the ground as tiny particles. The rest are dissolved by the moisture in the atmosphere. When it rains, these chemicals come down, too. This is called acid rain (above). It damages trees and other plants, and poisons the soil. Eventually acid rain drains into rivers and lakes, where it kills many fish.

Q Why are some insects called pests?

A Some insects harm people or crops. The Colorado beetle and the mint-leaf beetle damage food crops. The death-watch beetle destroys timber in buildings. The mosquito carries diseases.

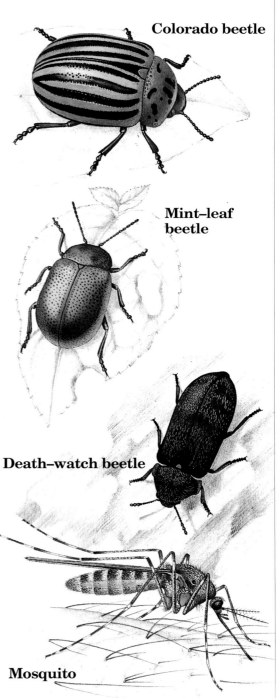

Colorado beetle

Mint–leaf beetle

Death–watch beetle

Mosquito

ANIMAL BEHAVIOR

Q How do musk oxen protect their young?

A When threatened by enemies, such as wolves, a herd of musk oxen (right) form a line facing them, or form a circle with the calves in the middle (below). Big males may dash out and jab the attackers with their huge, powerful, curved horns.

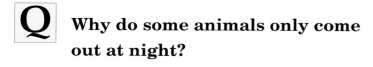

Q Why do some animals only come out at night?

A Animals that only come out at night are called nocturnal. They may be nocturnal in order to catch other nocturnal animals or to avoid daytime predators, or both. Nocturnal animals often have large eyes and good eyesight. They also need a sharp sense of smell and good hearing to listen for danger.

Q How do chimps show their moods?

A Scientists have shown that chimps (left) show their moods through their facial expressions. The shape of the mouth, and whether or not the teeth are bared, are important signals. From top to bottom, the chimps are showing a desire to play, begging for food, intense fear and, lastly, anxiety.

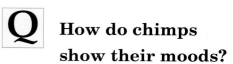

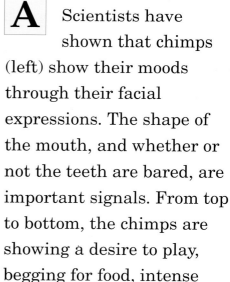

Q How does the honeyguide get its name?

A Honeyguides (below) live in Africa and India and are so called because they lead honey badgers and humans to the nests of wild bees using a series of calls. After the nest has been raided for honey, the bird gets the chance to feed on bee grubs from the open nest.

Q Why do animals defend their territory?

A Not all animals have territories, but many do. If food is limited, the animal may defend a territory to guard its food supply. With other species, such as these cassowaries (right), the males fight over a territory in which to nest and rear their young. Territorial animals know exactly where the boundaries of their own territory lie.

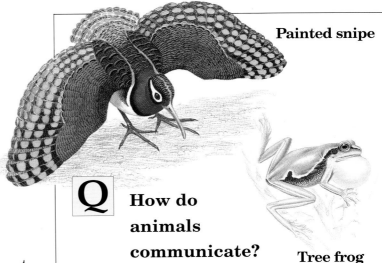

Painted snipe

Q How are young cuckoos reared?

A A female cuckoo (below) lays an egg in the nest of another bird and takes away one of the host's eggs to make room for it. The host bird has the task of feeding and rearing the young cuckoo. As it grows up, the young cuckoo pushes the host bird's eggs and young from the nest. By the time it is ready to leave the nest, the young cuckoo may be several times the size of its long-suffering foster parent.

Q How do animals communicate?

Tree frog

A Animals signal to each other mainly by using visual signals, such as shape or color, and by sound. Birds such as the painted snipe have showy wings which they fan out to make an impression. Many birds sing to mark their territories or attract a mate. Most frogs produce a croaking song to mark their territories or attract a mate.

NATURE

PETS

Q Who were the first people to keep cats as pets?

A The first people to keep cats (right) were probably the ancient Egyptians, over 3,000 years ago. Cats caught the mice, rats, and other vermin that raided the grain supplies. The cats were well cared for and became pets. In the end, they were worshiped as part of the Egyptian religion. Anyone who killed a cat would be sentenced to death. Some dead cats were even turned into mummies.

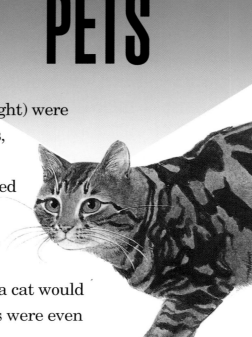

Q Why do some rabbits have drooping ears?

A This brown-and-gray lop-eared rabbit has very long, drooping ears. Lops have been specially bred over several centuries by mating does (female rabbits) and bucks (male rabbits) with long ears. Other rabbits (such as chinchillas) are bred to have long fur.

Q Which is the biggest scent hound in the world?

A The biggest of the scent hounds is the bloodhound (right). It has an extremely good sense of smell, more than a million times better than a human's, and is used to track criminals. Hounds are often bred with particular characteristics to help them hunt their prey. Otterhounds, for example, are excellent swimmers, and beagles are bred for stamina, enabling them to run long distances.

Otterhound

Beagle

Bloodhound

Q How quickly do mice breed?

A A female mouse is ready to have babies when she is seven weeks old. Three weeks after this, she could give birth to as many as ten young. She may go on producing new litters of babies every 20 to 30 days. In one year, a single mouse could have more than 100 babies!

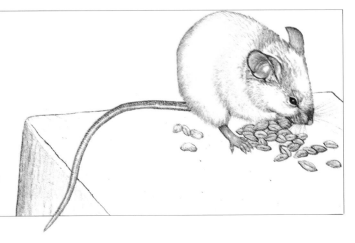

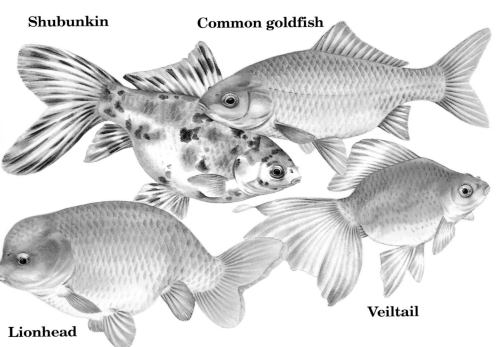

Shubunkin

Common goldfish

Lionhead

Veiltail

Q How did budgerigars get their name?

A Budgerigars (below) derived their name from the Australian Aboriginals. The Aboriginals like to catch and eat this wild bird, so they call it "betcherrygah," which means "good cockatoo." Budgerigars are popular as cage birds. They are brightly colored and can be taught to mimic the human voice.

Q How many kinds of goldfish are there?

A Goldfish (above) are related to the wild carp. The Chinese have bred carp in ponds for over 2,000 years. They probably picked out the red- and gold-colored fish and kept them as pets. There are now more than 150 different varieties of goldfish and its close relative, the koi carp. The shubunkin is covered with gray, gold, red, or blue patches, with black markings. The common goldfish is very hardy and can live through very cold winters, even if the water ices over. Some goldfish have been bred to have special features. The lionhead has a swelling on top of its head. The veiltail has a long double tail which hangs down like a veil. Other varieties have bubbles on either side of the head, or scales that are almost invisible.

NATURE

PETS

Q Where do canaries come from?

A In the wild, canaries (above) are found on the Canary Islands off North Africa and on the islands of the Azores and Madeira. They have been kept for more than 400 years because they can sing. Most captive birds are bright yellow, but breeding in captivity has produced a wide range of different colors. Their wild relatives are a duller olive-green color.

Q Do pet mice have wild relatives?

A Domesticated pet mice are all descended from the wild house mouse. This animal has lived alongside humans for more than 10,000 years, ever since people began to store grain and other foods. Mice have been kept as pets for several centuries, and a range of color varieties (right) has been bred.

Q What is a Manx cat?

A The Manx cat (above) is a very distinctive breed which is best known for its lack of tail. It first came from the Isle of Man, an island in the Irish Sea. Manx cats have long legs for their size, with thickset bodies. Their color is like that of a tabby or wild cat, with stripes and blotches of various shades of brown and gray-brown. Manx cats are popular as a show breed and are often kept as pets.

Q How many breeds of dogs are there?

A There are over 300 different breeds of dogs, and each country has its own system of grouping them. In the UK and Australia the main groups are: hounds, terriers, toys, gun, working, and utility. In the US dogs are also grouped into sporting and nonsporting. European countries use different groupings.

Bouvier des Flandres (working)

American foxhound (hound)

Q Are there different breeds of rabbit?

A There are many different breeds and varieties of rabbit, all descended from the wild rabbit. About 2,000 years ago, the Romans brought rabbits from their native Spain, Portugal, and southern France to raise them for their meat. Rabbits now live in many parts of the world. People also breed rabbits for their fur and for show.

Q What is a Persian cat?

A A Persian (right) is the best-known breed of long-haired cat. It was first bred in Europe in the 1800s by crossing cats imported from Persia (now Iran) and from Angora in Turkey. The breed has a long, silky coat and a broad head. A Persian cat's legs are short, but the body is broad and robust. Although this example is black and white, Persians come in several different colors.

**Irish setter
(gun dog)**

**Great dane
(utility)**

**Lakeland terrier
(terrier)**

**Chihuahua
(toy)**

FARM ANIMALS

Q What is the most popular cart-horse?

A The Percheron (left) is the most popular cart-horse breed in the world. It is named after Perche, the region of France where it was first developed and used. Standing more than 16.1 hands high, this gentle giant can pull immense loads without much effort. It was originally used for pulling heavy loads but today is just as popular as a show horse.

Q How are beef and dairy cattle different?

A Dairy cattle, such as this Friesian and Dairy Shorthorn, are lighter in build than beef cattle. The udders are big so that they can hold large volumes of milk. Before a dairy cow can produce milk, she has to give birth to a calf. After the birth, she continues to produce milk for up to 10 months or so. Dairy cows are usually milked twice a day.

Berkshire

Duroc

Q What meats do pigs provide?

A Pigs are reared for their meat, which is either eaten fresh as pork, or in cured form as bacon and ham. Different pig breeds serve different needs. The Duroc, Berkshire, and Saddleback are primarily pork breeds, while the Tamworth is a bacon breed.

Tamworth

Saddleback

Q Why are there different cattle breeds?

A Different breeds of cattle are suited to different climates around the world. The most successful breed of beef cattle is the Hereford. It is ideal for cool climates. For hot climates, breeds such as the Kankrej are ideal. It is popular in India. The Santa Gertrudis also thrives in hot places and is widely farmed in Texas.

Santa Gertrudis

Kankrej

Hereford

Q Why do people raise chickens?

A People keep chickens (right) for three main reasons: for their meat, for their eggs, and lastly for show. There are many different breeds. The Leghorn is the best egg-laying breed, while the Barnvelder is kept for meat.

Leghorn   Barnvelder

Q How long have people kept goats?

A Goats (right) have been kept as herd animals for at least 9,000 years. They are bred for their meat, milk, and skins. In some countries goats are used to carry loads and to pull small carts. In many countries, goat numbers are very high and they damage wild plant life by overgrazing.

Q What is sheep wool used for?

A The quality of sheep wool varies from breed to breed and can be used for a variety of purposes. The wool from the German Blackface is fine and makes excellent cloth. Wool from the Corriedale is coarse and springy and is used for tweeds and carpets.

Corriedale

German Blackface

PLANT KINGDOM

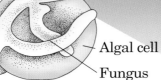

Algal cell

Fungus

Q What are lichens?

A Lichens (above) are strange plants. They are made up of algal cells, surrounded by a fungus. The same alga can live alone, but the fungus needs the alga to survive, because the alga can make food from sunlight energy. Lichens live on stones and trees and grow slowly.

Q Why are seaweeds slimy?

A Seaweeds (right) are simple plants that grow on the seashore. There are lots of different types, but most feel slimy to the touch. This is because there is a jellylike layer on the seaweed surface. This keeps the plants supple and prevents the seaweed from being damaged by the waves.

Q What are fungi?

A Fungi belong to a group of organisms separate from plants and animals. Unlike plants, they have no green pigment and cannot make their own food. The main part of a large fungus is a huge network of tiny threads in the ground. These take up food from dead plants and animals in the soil. At certain times of year, mushrooms and toadstools spring up from the threads and scatter spores that will grow into new fungi.

Fly agaric

Blusher

Cage fungus

Bracket fungus

Earthball

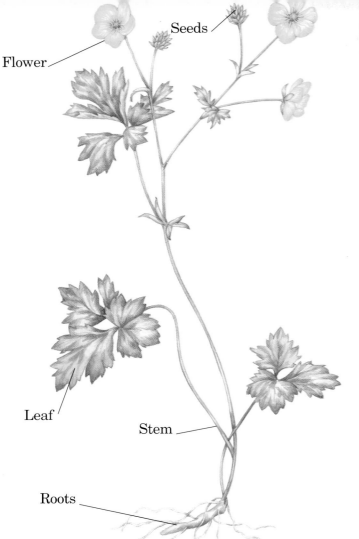

Flower

Seeds

Leaf

Stem

Roots

Q Which plants produce cones?

A Plants that produce cones are called conifers (below). Conifers often grow as large trees which are themselves cone-shaped in outline. Cones are the parts of the conifer used for reproduction, so there are male and female cones. Male cones produce pollen which is carried by the wind to fertilize the female cone. This then develops and matures. Seeds form between the hard, protective scales of the cone and are released when ripe.

Pine cone

Fir cone

Conifer tree

Q What are the parts of a flowering plant called?

A A flowering plant (above) usually has roots anchoring it in the soil. These take up water and nutrients. Above ground, a stem carries these to the leaves. The leaves use sunlight energy to make food. At the ends of the stem are flowers, the reproductive parts. Once fertilized, the flowers produce fruits and seeds.

Q How is timber cut from a tree trunk?

A A felled tree trunk is first stripped of its branches. It is then cut lengthwise in an ordered way so that no timber is wasted. First, two sides of the trunk are cut to produce thin planks of wood. Then the central part of the tree trunk is cut into thicker lengths of wood suitable for building work.

NATURE

PLANT LIFE

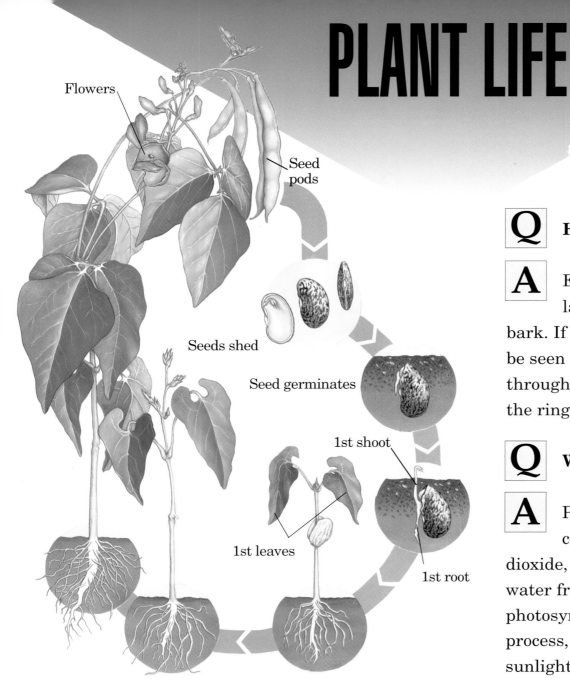

Flowers

Seed pods

Seeds shed

Seed germinates

1st shoot

1st leaves

1st root

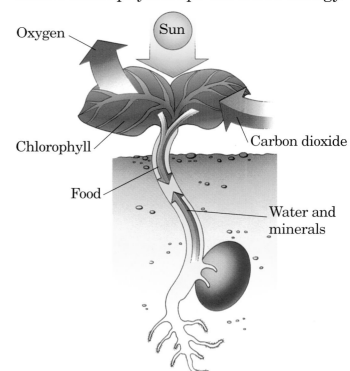

Q How does a plant complete its life cycle?

A Every year, plants (above) produce large numbers of seeds which fall to the ground. Many die, but some will germinate. Tiny roots and shoots grow from the seed and soon the plant increases in size. As the plant grows larger, more and more leaves are produced and eventually flowers appear. Pollen from male flowers fertilizes female flowers and the base of the flower begins to swell. It is here that this year's seeds are being made, completing the plant's life cycle.

Q How can you tell a tree's age?

A Every year a tree grows a new layer of wood just beneath the bark. If a tree is cut down, the layers can be seen as rings in the cross-section through the stump (above). By counting the rings you can tell its age.

Q Why do plants need sunlight?

A Plants make their own food by combining a gas called carbon dioxide, which they get from the air, with water from the soil. This process is called photosynthesis (below). To power the process, the plant uses the energy of sunlight. A green pigment in the leaves called chlorophyll traps the Sun's energy.

Oxygen

Sun

Chlorophyll

Carbon dioxide

Food

Water and minerals

Q Which plants eat animals?

A Venus's-flytraps and pitcher plants (right) can absorb nutrients from animals. Venus fly traps have leaves which trap insects and digest them. Pitcher plants have flask-shaped leaves in which water collects. Insects fall in, drown and decay.

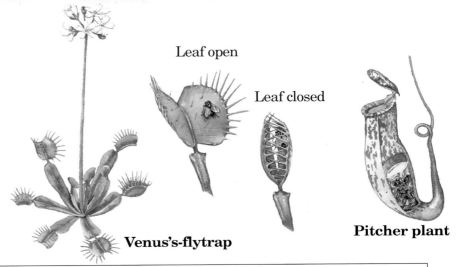

Leaf open

Leaf closed

Venus's-flytrap

Pitcher plant

Q What are fruit "pips"?

A Fruit "pips" are the seeds of the plant that produced the fruit. There are many types of fruit, and most are juicy and nutritious. Many animals eat them. The seed may be swallowed whole and passed out in the animal's droppings later on. In this way, the plant has its seeds scattered, or dispersed.

Q Why do plants produce flowers?

A Plants produce flowers (below) to reproduce and create a new generation. Flowers bear the male and female parts. Many flowers have colors and scents that attract insects. The insects take male pollen to the female parts of other flowers. The pollen of some flowers is carried by the wind.

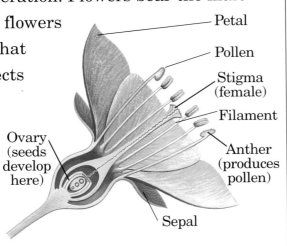

Petal

Pollen

Stigma (female)

Filament

Ovary (seeds develop here)

Anther (produces pollen)

Sepal

Fritillary

Clematis

Orchid

Silver birch

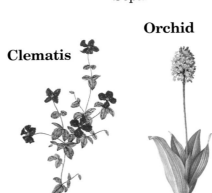

Q How do daffodils survive the winter?

A Daffodils have leaves and flowers above ground only for a few months each spring. During the winter they live as onionlike bulbs in the ground. The bulbs are full of food and are protected from winter frosts by the soil above them.

Bulb cross-section

NATURE

EARLY CIVILIZATIONS

Q How can we find out about ancient cities?

A Archaeologists dig up the ruins of ancient cities (below). They divide the site where the city once stood into squares. Each square is given a number. The archaeologists remember the original position of anything they discover by noting the number of the square they find it in. In this way, they can build up a picture of what the city once looked like.

Q Why was Babylon important?

A Babylon (below) stood on the River Euphrates in Mesopotamia (now part of Iraq). At first it was one of a series of small cities. Then Babylon grew in power. By 1700 BC, it controlled an empire, known as Babylonia, which covered the southern part of Mesopotamia. Much of the wealth Babylon gained from the empire was used for building. The Hanging Gardens were a series of irrigated gardens probably built high up on the terraces of ziggurats.

Q What was a ziggurat?

A A ziggurat was an artificial hill built in a series of layers, or platforms. At the top was a temple. To build a ziggurat (below), huge mounds of clay were strengthened with reeds and covered with bricks. Ziggurats were built in the cities of Mesopotamia from about 2500 BC to 500 BC and in ancient New World civilizations.

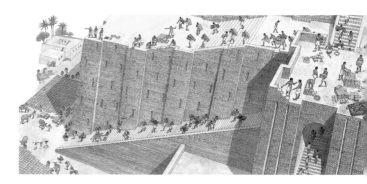

Q What was the Neolithic?

A This was a period in prehistory (a period where we have no written documents) during which agriculture became a way of life (above). People grew crops of wheat and barley and kept domestic cattle and sheep. Villages were few and scattered, and people rarely traveled more than a few days' walk from home. The Neolithic lasted from about 9000 BC to 3000 BC.

Q What were cylinder seals?

A These were cylinders, generally made of stone, that were used to roll clay over such things as jars, or locks to storehouses, to seal them. The cylinders were generally carved with a design. This meant that a pattern was produced when the clay was rolled out. Writing was often carved onto cylinders so that it could be transferred to clay tablets.

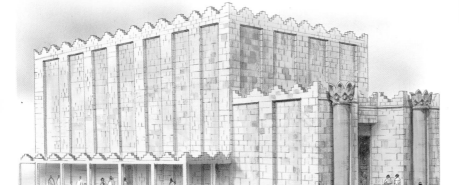

Q Who was Solomon?

A Solomon was king of Israel from approximately 970 BC to 922 BC. He was well known for his immense wealth and wisdom. He encouraged trade and Israel became rich. Solomon extended Israel's empire and started many building schemes, including the building of the first temple at Jerusalem (left), and a palace for himself and his queen.

ANCIENT EGYPT

Q How did the Egyptians use chariots in battle?

A The Egyptian army began to use chariots after 1500 BC. The chariots were made of wood and leather, and were drawn by two horses. They carried two men. While a charioteer drove, a soldier behind would fire arrows at the enemy.

Q What was life like in the Egyptian army?

A The picture below shows the army of Rameses II, ruler of Egypt from 1290 BC to 1224 BC, in camp. The chariot horses are tethered, and one chariot is being repaired. A band of foot soldiers is being trained. The soldiers are carrying spears and axes with bronze heads, and bows made from two antelope horns tied together. Egyptian soldiers also fought with scimitars, which were curved swords.

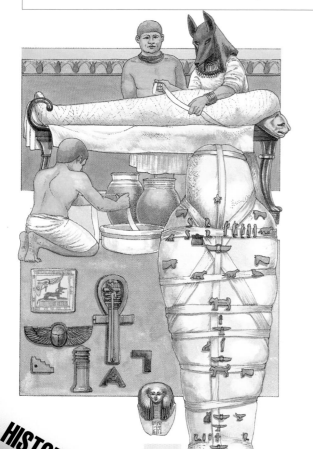

Q What is a mummy?

A The Egyptians believed that people's spirits lived on after death. Because the spirits were attached to the dead body, the body had to be preserved so that it could enjoy the afterlife (left). First, the brain was taken out through the nose, and the heart and other organs were cut out. The body was dried, stuffed with linen and spices, and treated with resin and perfumed oils. Then it was wrapped in long linen bandages. At this stage, it is known to us as a mummy. The chief embalmer wore the mask of Anubis, the jackal god who protected the dead. Small charms called amulets were placed inside the layers of wrappings to protect each part of the body. Finally, the mummies were sealed in grand and costly tombs.

Q What did Egyptian boats look like?

A This boat carried cargoes up and down the River Nile. It had a huge sail, which was wider than it was tall. One man stood in the stern, directing the boat by moving the double steering oars. There were lookout posts at each end of the boat.

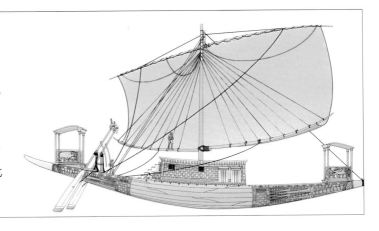

Q What was life like in an Egyptian town?

A Egyptian houses were made of dried mud and built close together (left). Wet mats were spread across the floors to cool the air. Most of the housework, such as cooking and washing, was done outside. People often kept goats and geese in their backyards, as well as pet animals such as dogs, cats, and monkeys.

Q How were the pyramids built?

A Between 2630 BC and 1640 BC, Egyptian kings were buried in tombs inside huge pyramids. Stonemasons quarried, shaped, and smoothed blocks of stone. The blocks were then lashed to sleds. These were dragged over wooden rollers, which were kept damp to prevent friction. Mudbrick ramps were used to bring the stones up to where they were needed (below).

HISTORY

ANCIENT GREECE

Q What did a Greek soldier wear in battle?

A A Greek foot soldier (right) was called a hoplite. He wore a linen shirt with metal armor plates on the shoulders. A bronze breastplate covered his chest and stomach, and greaves (shin guards) covered his legs. He wore a bronze helmet with a tall crest on his head. The hoplite carried a shield and a spear. Around his waist was a belt with a short sword. Hoplites fought in close formation.

Q What was the Parthenon?

A The Parthenon (above) was a temple in Athens that honored the Greek goddess Athena. It was built between 447 BC and 432 BC on a hill called the Acropolis, above the city. The temple had 46 pillars, and was made of white marble. Its ruins still stand today.

Q What was a trireme?

A A trireme was a Greek warship (right). It was powered by 170 oarsmen who sat on three levels. Each level had oars of different lengths. The trireme sank enemy ships with a long ram built into its bow.

Q Why was the marketplace important?

A Each city in ancient Greece had its own government. In the 5th century BC, Athens was the most powerful of these cities, and controlled an empire. Its empire brought Athens trade 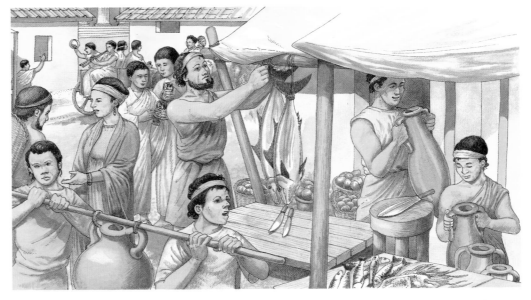 and prosperity, and the marketplace became an important part of city life. It was the city's public business area. Here, people would buy the food they needed. It was here, too, that politics might be discussed. Athens was the first democracy ever. This meant that each citizen could participate in how the city was governed. However, only free men who had been born in Athens were counted as citizens.

Q How was Greek pottery made?

A One person would shape the pot by hand (below), while another would paint it. The pots, which were made of clay, were decorated with scenes from daily life, or might show the deeds of gods, goddesses, and heroes.

Q What were Greek houses like?

A In the 5th century BC, wealthy Greeks had grand houses made of clay bricks, with stone or tile floors (above). There were separate rooms for eating, cooking, washing, and sleeping, built around an open courtyard. The poorer people lived in houses with only one or two rooms.

HISTORY

BIBLICAL TIMES

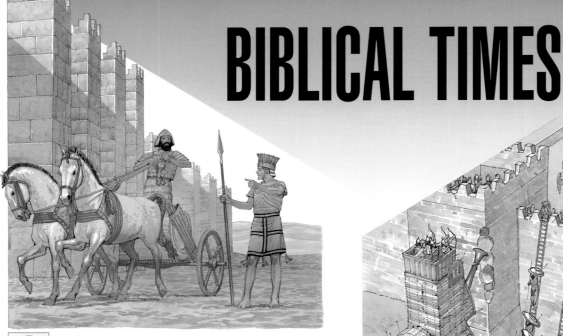

Q **Where was Canaan?**

A Canaan was the land we now know as Israel. In about 1250 BC, the Israelites, led by Joshua, invaded Canaan. The Canaanites were better armed and fought from horses and chariots (above), but the Israelites were able to defeat many Canaanite cities.

Q **How did Greek culture spread?**

A Alexander the Great was king of Greece from 336 BC to 323 BC. He conquered many lands (below), including the Bible lands of Syria and Egypt. The Hebrews who lived there began to translate their holy scriptures into Greek.

Q **Who were the Assyrians?**

A These were a people who built up a powerful empire from their homeland in Mesopotamia (now part of Iraq). They were enemies of the Hebrews from about 860 BC to 612 BC. The Assyrians were skilled in many areas of warfare. They used machines such as those shown above to capture fortified cities. The machines protected the soldiers while they knocked down the walls with battering rams. Other soldiers distracted the defenders by scaling the walls with long ladders.

Q Who was Herod the Great?

A Herod was king of Judea (a part of Israel) from about 37 BC to 4 BC. He had a number of palaces built for himself. The largest of these was the Upper Palace in Jerusalem (left), from which Herod governed.

Q Why was the Sea of Galilee important?

A The Sea of Galilee (in Israel) was rich in fish. Fishermen sailed in boats about 20 feet long. The fish were sold throughout the Roman Empire, bringing wealth to the region.

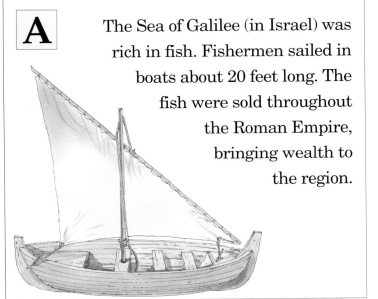

Q Why were carpenters important in Biblical times?

A Wood was the main material for making tools such as plows and yokes (above). Furniture was also made of wood. Jesus and his father, Joseph, are described as carpenters in the Bible.

Q What did Jerusalem look like in Old Testament times?

A Jerusalem (left) was founded sometime before 2000 BC. King David made it the Israelite capital in about 1000 BC. Jerusalem was surrounded by strong walls and contained fine palaces, but it remained comparatively small with narrow alleyways and poor housing. King David's son, Solomon, later built a temple and palace in the city.

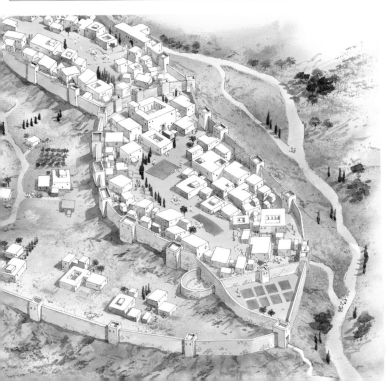

HISTORY

ANCIENT ROME

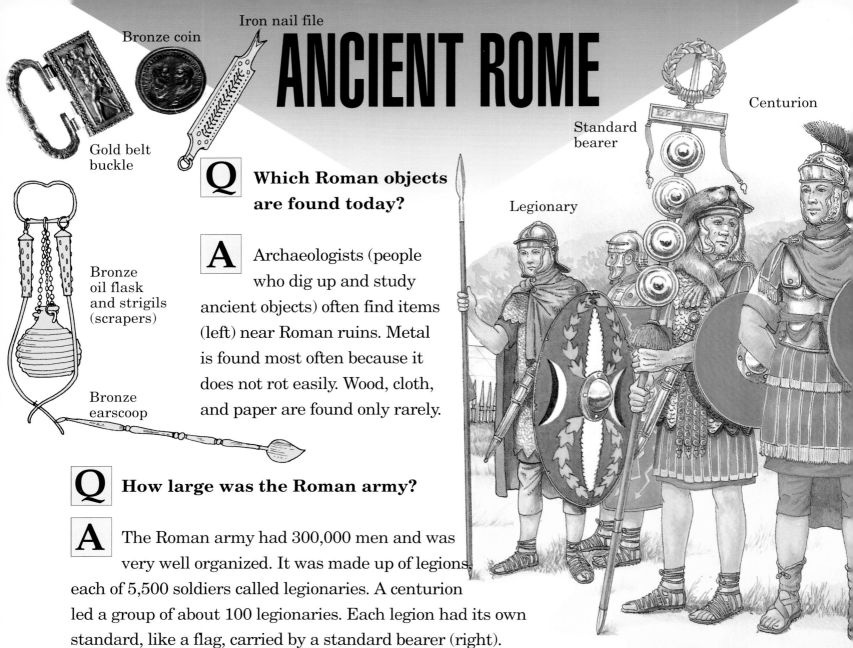

Bronze coin

Iron nail file

Gold belt buckle

Bronze oil flask and strigils (scrapers)

Bronze earscoop

Standard bearer

Centurion

Legionary

Q **Which Roman objects are found today?**

A Archaeologists (people who dig up and study ancient objects) often find items (left) near Roman ruins. Metal is found most often because it does not rot easily. Wood, cloth, and paper are found only rarely.

Q **How large was the Roman army?**

A The Roman army had 300,000 men and was very well organized. It was made up of legions, each of 5,500 soldiers called legionaries. A centurion led a group of about 100 legionaries. Each legion had its own standard, like a flag, carried by a standard bearer (right).

Q **How large was the Roman Empire?**

A In AD 211, the Roman Empire covered the land shown on this map (right). About 100 million people lived in the Roman Empire. The lands were divided into areas called provinces. Each province had a governor who collected the taxes, and kept law and order.

- town
— road
Roman empire AD211

0   800km
0   600mi

Eburacum
Londinium
Colonia Agrippina
ATLANTIC OCEAN
Moguntiacum
Augusta Treverorum
Augusta Vindelicorum
Burdigala
Lugdunum
Poetovio
Apulum
Narbo
Genua
Bononia
Troesmis
Oescus
Segovia
Tarraco
Salonae
Black Sea
Rome
Emerita Augusta
Byzantium
Sinope
Corduba
Thessalonica
Nicomedia
Tingi
Iol Caesarea
Athens
Ephesus
Caesarea
Carthage
Syracuse
Tarsus
Antiochia
Mediterranean Sea
Leptis Magna
Bostra
Caesarea
Cyrene
Alexandria

Q **How did the Romans protect themselves in battle?**

A To protect themselves from enemy spears and arrows, Roman legionaries would form a tortoise (below). A group of soldiers would crowd together and lock their shields to form four walls and a roof. It was called a tortoise because it looked like a tortoise's shell.

Roman tortoise

Q **What did the Romans build?**

Temple

A The Romans were skillful engineers and architects. They built many fine buildings as well as temples to worship their gods. This cross-section through an amphitheater shows how the arches were designed to carry the enormous weight of the building. The Romans are also famous for their road building.

Amphitheater

Road

Q **What ships did the Romans build?**

A The Romans built merchant ships to carry food and other goods, and warships. The merchant ship was broad and deep so that it could carry thousands of containers of goods. The war galley was long and narrow so that it could travel fast and also turn quickly. It used oarsmen as well as sails, so it could move quickly even when there was no wind.

A small warship

A medium-sized merchant ship

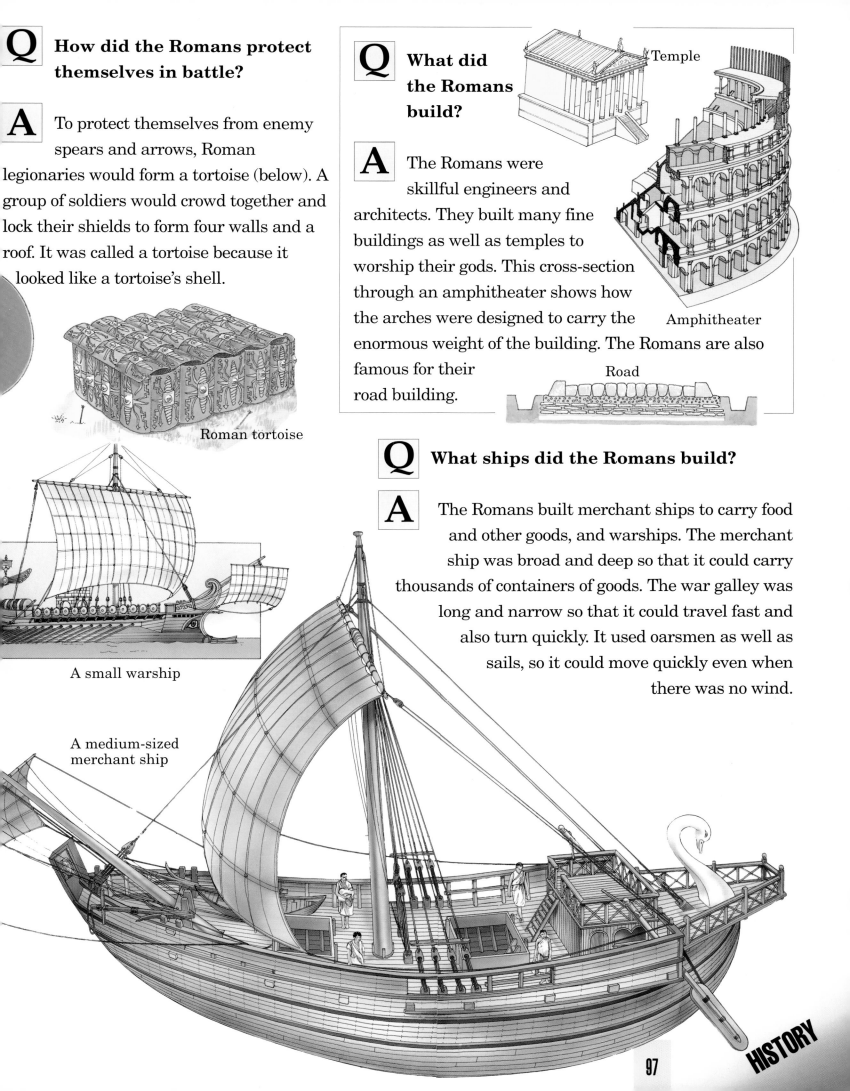

HISTORY

MIDDLE AGES

Q Who was buried at Sutton Hoo?

A In AD 625, the Saxon King Raedwald died. He was buried at Sutton Hoo, in Suffolk, England. The king was laid out in a wooden ship, 88 feet long (below), which people believed would take him to the next world. Spears, dishes, coins, armor, and a stringed instrument called a lyre were found inside the ship. Also found were silver and gold ornaments, such as these gold clasps (right). The ship and the king were buried under a huge mound of earth. The ship was rediscovered in 1938.

Q What was the Domesday Book?

A William of Normandy conquered England in 1066. In 1086, he ordered a survey of all his English lands to check that he was receiving the rent and taxes to which he was entitled. His officers traveled around the kingdom asking a series of questions, such as the name of each estate and who owned it (right). The answers were written in the Domesday Book. It gives us a detailed picture of what life was like in the Middle Ages.

Q How were cathedrals built in the 12th century?

A During the 12th century, a new style of church architecture was introduced which meant that buildings were much larger and more elaborate than before. This style was known as Gothic architecture (left). The inside of the cathedral was enlarged by building aisles of columns on each side. Arches were built on the outside of cathedrals to support the enormous weight of the roof. Each wall was pierced with windows, which let in light and made the walls lighter.

Q What were the Crusades?

A The Crusades were religious wars fought between the 11th and 13th centuries. They were fought to win back the Holy Lands from non-Christians. The First Crusade began in 1076, when Palestine was captured by Turkish Muslims. The crusading armies were usually led by knights on horseback. Foot soldiers fought with spears and crossbows.

Q What was Paris like in the 14th century?

A The center of the city of Paris (above) was an island in the River Seine, joined to the rest of the city by bridges. Barges brought goods down the river from all over France. Most houses were made of wood, but the grander buildings were stone. Grandest of all was the cathedral of Notre-Dame with its twin towers.

EARLY AFRICA

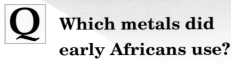

Q Which metals did early Africans use?

A Iron was used in Africa from about 200 BC, and copper from 500 BC. Beautiful statues were a special art form in the Benin Empire (AD 1200–1700) in West Africa. They were cast in bronze or brass. This one (left) shows in detail a hunter returning home. He has an antelope slung over his shoulders with its legs tied.

Q What was the Great Trek?

A In 1806 the British captured the Dutch Cape Colony in southern Africa. Many Dutch farmers, called Boers, resented British rule. In 1836, they set off northeastward with their families on a Great Trek. They settled north of the Orange and Vaal rivers. The wealthy republics they founded now form part of South Africa.

Q What was Great Zimbabwe?

A The modern state of Zimbabwe (in southern Africa) is named after the ruins of some huge stone-walled enclosures that were found in the hills of south-central Zimbabwe. Great Zimbabwe (above) was where the ruler of the city lived, and was the center of religious life for his people. This is how it would have looked in the 15th century.

Q What were early African villages like?

A South of the Sahara, Africa was populated by hundreds of different tribes, each with their own culture. Whatever their way of life, the villages, such as this one in Chad (left), had much in common. Houses were built of wood, clay, or grass. Round huts were very common, each being used for a single purpose such as cooking or sleeping. Huts were usually grouped around a courtyard in which a single family lived. Many Africans still live in traditional villages and huts.

Q What was the East Coast Trade?

A The east coast of Africa was for a long time an important source of trade in gold, ivory, and other goods. The first to exploit it were the Arabs, who sailed as far south as Madagascar from about AD 700 onward. In 1498 Portuguese ships (right) began to take part in the rich East Coast Trade. Wars were fought between the Arabs and Portuguese for control of ports and sea routes. Other European nations, including the Spanish, Dutch, and English, also exploited the trade.

Q Who were the first people to live in America?

EARLY AMERICA

A About 25,000 years ago there was a bridge of land between America and Asia. This was the time of the last ice age. Hunters (below) crossed over from Asia in small bands, following animals such as caribou and bison. Slowly, these settlers spread southward into the heart of the continent.

Q When did Inuits first live in America?

A Inuits (North American Eskimos) began to move into America from Asia between 4000 BC and 3000 BC. As they traveled, they built temporary houses. In winter, these were made of snow and are called igloos (below).

Q What kind of houses did the Plains Indians live in?

A In the 1400s, many Indians of the Great Plains were farmers. They built large, dome-shaped houses called lodges (right). A lodge had a wooden frame, covered with soil and turf. Entry was through a covered passage. Inside, there was a fireplace in the center of the lodge. A hole in the roof above let out the smoke. Around the walls were wooden platforms that were used as beds or seats. Before the introduction of the horse by the Spanish, the Plains Indians used dogs for hunting.

Q What was the capital of the Aztec Empire?

A The Aztecs ruled a huge empire in Mexico from AD 1345 to AD 1521. Their capital city was Tenochtitlan, built on swampy islands in Lake Texcoco. Over 300,000 people lived there. Goods were brought to the great markets by a system of canals, and each day vast crowds came to trade. This picture (below) shows the ceremonial center of the city, with Aztec nobles and warriors. The temple of Quetzalcoatl is before them and, beyond it, the double temple pyramid dedicated to the gods of war and rain.

Q What was the Pyramid of the Sun?

A The Pyramid of the Sun was the largest and oldest building in the Mexican city of Teotihuacan, which was built in AD 150. Standing over 230 feet high, the pyramid had a flat roof on which there was probably a temple dedicated to the Sun god.

Q How did the Incas travel around their empire?

A The Inca Empire stretched for nearly 2,500 miles along the west coast of South America. The Incas built a network of roads across their empire to transport goods, move troops, and send messages (left). The roads were made as straight as possible, but zigzagged up steep slopes. Bridges, hung from cables of twisted plant stems, were fixed across ravines and rivers. There were no wheeled vehicles, so most people walked. However, important officers were carried in litters (a type of chair carried on poles).

HISTORY

GREAT EXPLORERS

Q Where did Christopher Columbus land when he discovered America in 1492?

A Columbus sailed from Spain across the Atlantic in his ship the *Santa Maria* (below). He was trying to reach China. Instead, in 1492, he landed on the island of San Salvador in the Caribbean Sea.

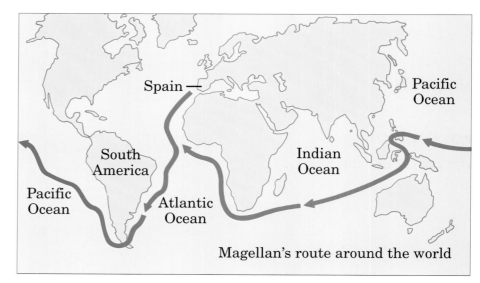

Q Who was Marco Polo?

A Marco Polo was an Italian who traveled from Venice to China with his father and uncle. He arrived in China in 1275 and stayed for 17 years. He worked for the Chinese ruler Kublai Khan (above). He described his travels in a famous book.

Q Why was Ferdinand Magellan famous?

A In 1519, Ferdinand Magellan, a Portuguese navigator, sailed around the tip of South America, into the Pacific Ocean (right). Magellan himself was killed in 1521, but one of his ships completed the first round-the-world voyage.

Spain

Pacific Ocean

Pacific Ocean

South America

Atlantic Ocean

Indian Ocean

Magellan's route around the world

Q Who led the first expedition to the South Pole?

A Roald Amundsen of Norway landed his party on Antarctica in 1911. Amundsen and four men started for the South Pole on sleds drawn by dogs. They reached the Pole in less than two months (right). The journey back was even quicker, and everyone returned safely. Soon afterward, Robert F. Scott's British expedition also reached the Pole. But none of the five men survived the return trip.

Q Who was the first European to cross Africa from east to west?

A In 1874, H. M. Stanley (above) set out with 350 others from Bagamoyo on Africa's east coast. After exploring Lake Victoria, the expedition reached the Congo River. Despite attacks from hostile tribes, they followed the river all the way to the sea on the west coast. The great journey took 999 days. Only 114 people survived.

INDUSTRIAL REVOLUTION

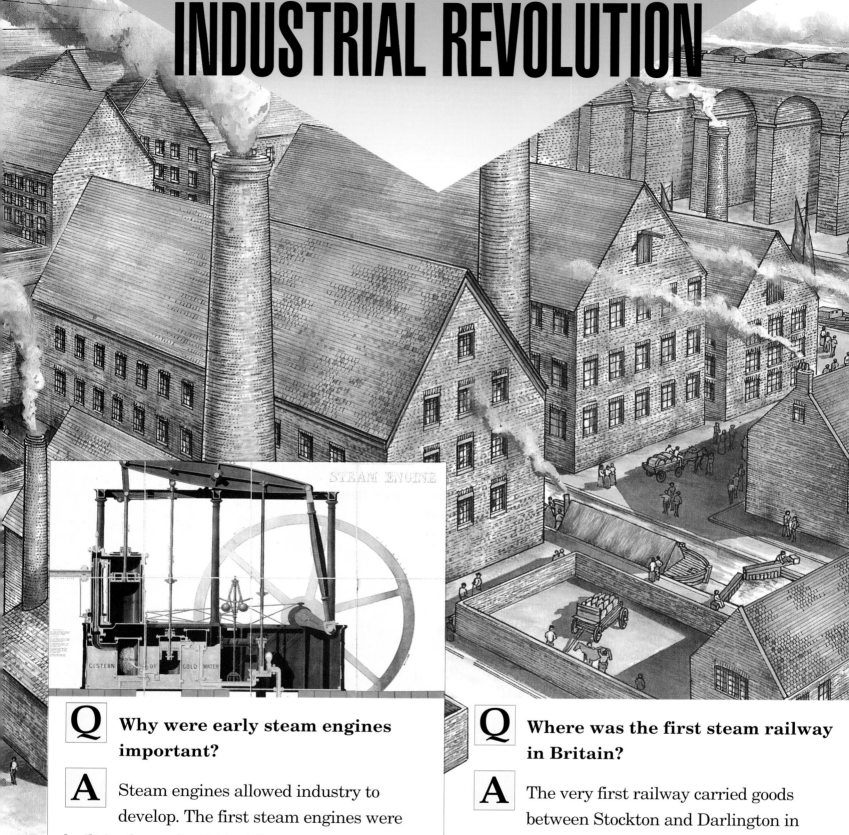

STEAM ENGINE

CISTERN OF COLD WATER

Q Why were early steam engines important?

A Steam engines allowed industry to develop. The first steam engines were built in the early 1700s. They were used to pump water out of mines. In the 1780s, James Watt produced a steam engine that was much more powerful. This was used to power many machines, including spinning and weaving looms, and farm plows and threshers.

Q Where was the first steam railway in Britain?

A The very first railway carried goods between Stockton and Darlington in northern England. It was opened in 1825, and was followed in 1830 by a line between Manchester and Liverpool (right). This carried both goods and passengers.

Q Why was the first seed drill so important?

A Jethro Tull made the first seed drill in 1701. Before this, seed had been scattered by hand. The drill sowed the seed in straight lines, so there was less waste and the crop was easier to weed and cut.

Q What was the Industrial Revolution?

A The Industrial Revolution is the name given to a time of great change in Britain. Before the 1700s, people made goods in small quantities, by hand. During the 1700s, machines were invented that made goods much more quickly. Manufacturing industry had begun, and it soon spread around the world. Factories were built (above), and people moved from the country to the towns to work in them.

Q Which new goods were made in the Industrial Revolution?

A New spinning and weaving machines enabled the textile industry to develop, and cheaper clothes could be made. Basic products such as iron and steel were used, and the steel industry developed. New methods were found to make many important products, such as rails, pans, and muskets. At the same time, machine tools, such as the lathe, were invented.

WORLD WARS

Q **When were aircraft first used in battle?**

A Aircraft were used in battle for the first time during the First World War (1914–18). At first they were used to spy on enemy troops, but later guns and bombs were fitted. The triplane (above) was preferred to the biplane because it had greater lift and was easier to maneuver.

Q **What caused the outbreak of the First World War?**

A The murder of the heir to the Austrian throne, Archduke Franz Ferdinand, on June 28, 1914, finally started the First World War (1914–18). He was killed by a Serb, causing Austria to declare war on Serbia.

Q **What was trench warfare?**

A During the First World War, soldiers dug trenches (below) as protection against weapons such as machine guns and heavy artillery. Soldiers would live in the trenches for weeks on end. Attacks were often made from the trenches.

Q **Who led the Germans during the Second World War?**

A Adolf Hitler (left) led the Germans during the Second World War (1939–45). His aim was to build a German Empire. In September 1938 he forced Austria to merge with Germany, and Czechoslovakia to hand territory over to him. The following year, he declared war on Poland. This caused Britain and France to declare war against the Germans, but by the end of 1940, France was defeated and Britain isolated. The Americans joined the war against the Germans in 1941, following an attack on Pearl Harbor by Japan (who was allied to Germany), and Germany was finally defeated in 1945.

Q **What kind of weapons were used in the Second World War?**

A Aircraft played a decisive role in many battles, while armored tanks made land warfare highly mobile. Aircraft carriers enabled aircraft to attack from the sea.

Tank

Allies
Central powers
Neutral

Russia

United Kingdom

German Empire

France

Austro-Hungarian Empire

Spain

Italy

Serbia

Ottoman Empire

Q **What were the main alliances during the First World War?**

A The two main alliances during the First World War were those who fought with the German Empire (known as the Central Powers), and those who fought against the German Empire (known as the Allies). Neutral countries did not fight on either side.

Q **What was D-Day?**

A D-Day was a code name used in the Second World War. It was the name given to the date when 130,000 troops from the British and American armies were due to land in France and liberate it from the Germans (right). The date was changed several times due to bad weather, but D-Day eventually took place on June 6, 1944.

Spitfire

Stuka

Aircraft carrier

HISTORY

HUMAN BODY

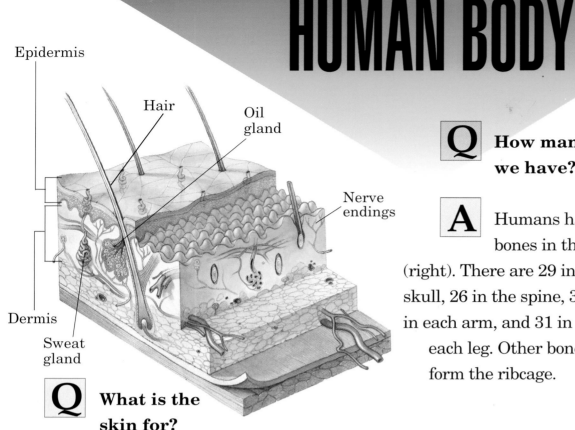

Epidermis

Hair

Oil gland

Nerve endings

Dermis

Sweat gland

Q **What is the skin for?**

A The skin (above) is the protective outer covering of our body. It contains nerve endings, which detect pain; sweat glands, which keep the body cool; and hair. It also prevents the body from losing too much water.

Q **How do muscles work?**

A There are more than 600 muscles in the body (right). Most of them move parts of the body or help it stay upright. Muscles cannot push, they can only pull. Many of them work in pairs, attached to bones by tendons. One muscle tightens and becomes shorter, pulling the bone after it. If it relaxes, and the other muscle tightens, the bone moves back.

Q **How many bones do we have?**

A Humans have 206 bones in their bodies (right). There are 29 in the skull, 26 in the spine, 32 in each arm, and 31 in each leg. Other bones form the ribcage.

Skull

Collarbone

Ribcage

Pelvis

Femur (thighbone)

Spine

Tibia and Fibula (shinbones)

Chest muscles used in breathing

Neck muscles turn head

Upper arm muscles bend and straighten elbow

Q **What is inside a bone?**

A Bones are not solid. They have a strong outer layer of compact bone, with lightweight, spongy bone inside. In the center is the soft marrow, which makes new red cells for the blood.

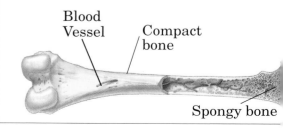

Blood Vessel

Compact bone

Spongy bone

Q What are veins and arteries?

A When blood leaves the lungs, it carries oxygen. This blood travels along vessels called arteries. The body absorbs the oxygen, and the blood travels back to the heart through veins (below).

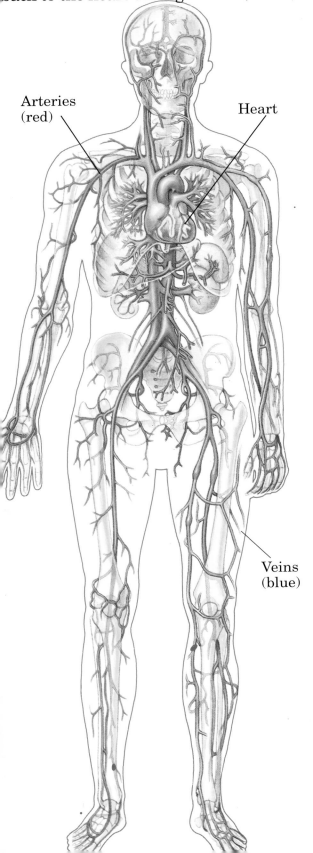

Arteries (red)

Heart

Veins (blue)

Q How does the heart work?

A The heart is a muscular pump. Oxygen-rich blood from the lungs enters the left side of the heart and is pumped to the organs. Veins carry the blood back to the right side of the heart. The blood is then pumped back to the lungs.

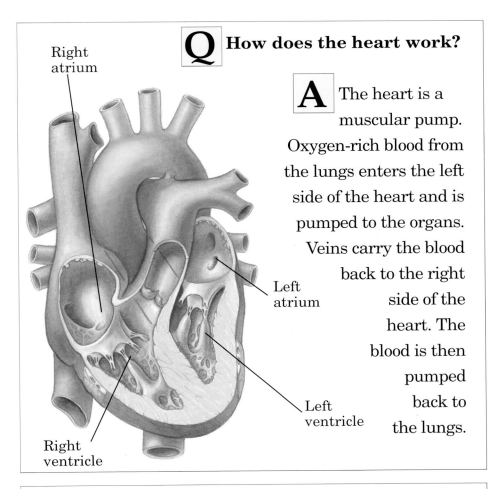

Right atrium

Left atrium

Left ventricle

Right ventricle

Q How do our joints work?

A Joints are the places where bones move against each other. Shoulders and hips have ball-and-socket joints. These allow movement in any direction. Elbows have hinge joints, which allow them to move backward and forward. A pivot joint allows the head to turn sideways.

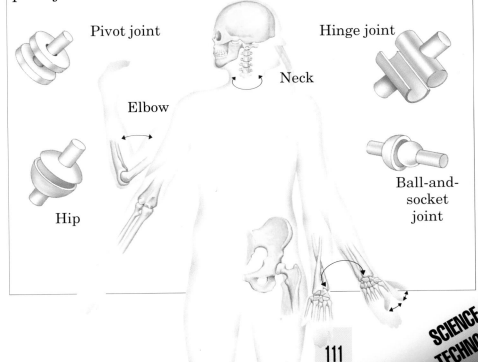

Pivot joint

Hinge joint

Neck

Elbow

Hip

Ball-and-socket joint

SENSES & ORGANS

Q How do we breathe?

A Our bodies need oxygen, which they get from air breathed into the lungs. The lungs are made to expand by a big muscle called the diaphragm, and smaller muscles fixed to the ribs. The diaphragm pushes downward, while the other muscles lift up the ribcage. This draws air down into the lungs, where the oxygen is absorbed into the blood stream (right).

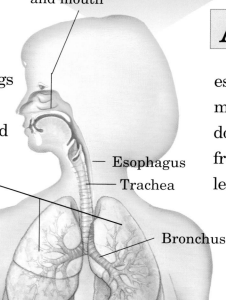

Air breathed in through nose and mouth

Esophagus

Lungs

Trachea

Bronchus

Diaphragm

Q How do our eyes see?

A When we look at something, light from it enters our eyes. The light is focused on the retina at the back of the eye by the lens. The optic nerves in the retina send a message to the brain, enabling us to "see."

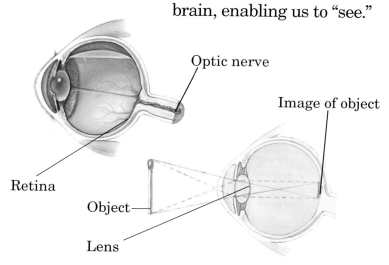

Optic nerve

Image of object

Retina

Object

Lens

Q Where does our food go?

A After the teeth chew the food, it is swallowed and goes down the esophagus into the stomach (below). It is mixed with digestive juices, which break it down. In the small intestine, nutrients from the food are absorbed. Waste matter leaves the body through the anus.

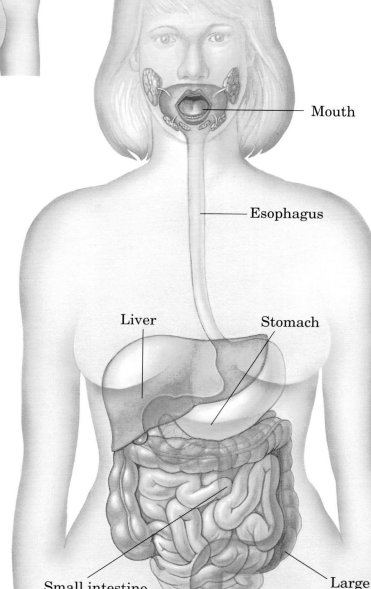

Mouth

Esophagus

Liver

Stomach

Small intestine

Large intesti

Anus

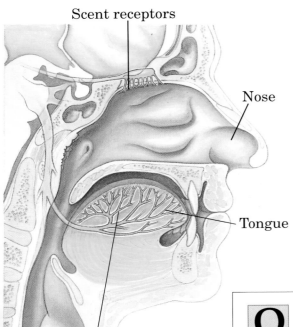

Scent receptors

Nose

Tongue

Taste receptors

Q How do we taste and smell?

A In the upper part of the nose are tiny scent receptors (left). When we sniff, molecules in the air are carried to these receptors. They sense what we are smelling. The tongue is covered with about 9,000 taste receptors, or taste buds. These sense what we are tasting. The taste buds are grouped in special areas on the tongue. Sweetness is tasted at the front, saltiness and sourness at the sides, and bitterness at the back.

Q How do our ears work?

A The outer ear collects sound waves, which pass through the eardrum and vibrate the tiny bones in the middle ear. These vibrations set the fluid in the cochlea in motion, shaking tiny hairs. Nerves attached to the hairs pass the message to the brain.

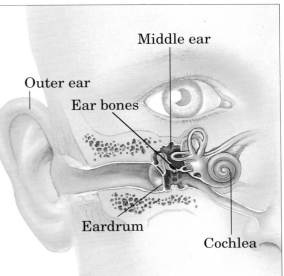

Outer ear

Middle ear

Ear bones

Eardrum

Cochlea

2 weeks

4 weeks

6 weeks

8 weeks

Baby

Uterus

Umbilical cord

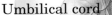

Q How does a baby develop during pregnancy?

A A baby's life begins when a male sperm joins a female egg. The sperm travels from a man into a woman's body. It joins with the egg to form a single cell, and starts to grow. After a week, the single cell has multiplied to more than 100 cells. After eight weeks, the baby has all its major organs (such as heart, liver, and lungs). The baby gets its food from its mother through the umbilical cord. After nine months, the baby is about 20 inches long (left). It is ready to be born.

SCIENCE OF LIFE

Plant cell

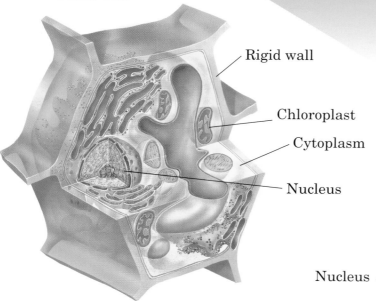

Rigid wall

Chloroplast

Cytoplasm

Nucleus

Nonrigid wall   **Animal cell**

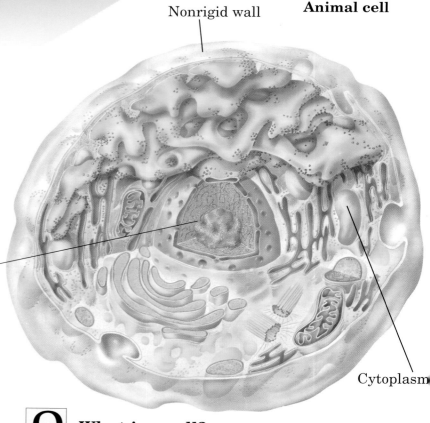

Nucleus

Cytoplasm

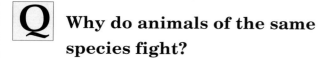

Q **Why do animals of the same species fight?**

A Animals fight others of their species for several reasons. They may be arguing over territory, or the right to be leader of their herd. Although many animals have powerful weapons, such as teeth, horns, or claws, few are ever killed in these contests. These two klipspringer antelopes are jabbing at each other with their sharp horns.

Q **What is a cell?**

A A cell (above) is the basic building block of almost every living thing. Plant cells have a rigid wall made of a material called cellulose. Animal cells do not have a rigid wall. Inside all cells is a fluid called cytoplasm, containing the nucleus and other small bodies. The nucleus is the cell's control center. The chloroplasts in plant cells help trap the energy from sunlight. The energy is used to turn carbon dioxide and water into food for the plant.

Q How do plants make seeds?

A Plants have male and female parts that join together to make seeds. A pollen grain travels from the male anther of one flower to the female stigma of another (right). The pollen is usually carried by an insect or the wind. It fertilizes an egg in the ovary, which becomes an embryo and then a seed. The seed will grow into a new plant.

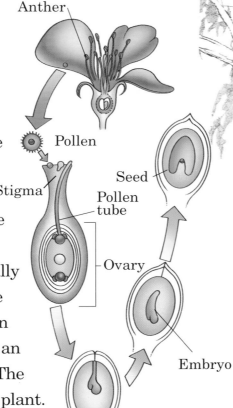

Anther

Pollen

Stigma

Pollen tube

Seed

Ovary

Embryo

Q How do racing pigeons find their way home?

A Racing pigeons and many other species of birds probably use more than one way of navigating. They can find their direction from the position of the Sun by day and the stars by night. They can also detect changes in the Earth's magnetic field as they fly over it. This tells them whether they are flying north, south, east, or west. Some birds find their way by smell.

Q Do animals live in families?

A Some animals live together in herds or flocks, but others live in small family groups. This is a family of tamarin monkeys (above). The older brothers and sisters carry and help groom the babies.

Q How do birds fly?

A These pictures (below) show a duck beating its wings once as it flies. The downstroke (left) lifts the bird up and propels it forward. On the upstroke (right) the feathers are opened to let air through.

SCIENCE & TECHNOLOGY

Hydrogen

Oxygen

Water molecule

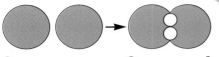

Oxygen atoms   **Oxygen molecule**

CHEMICALS & MATTER

Q What are molecules?

A A molecule (above) is the simplest part of a substance that can take part in chemical reactions. It is a group of two or more atoms linked together. The atoms may be the same or different. For example, a molecule of water is made of two hydrogen atoms linked to an oxygen atom. An oxygen molecule is made of two oxygen atoms linked together.

Q What is the difference between a mixture and a compound?

A If iron filings and sulfur (1) are mixed together (2), there is no chemical reaction and they can be separated again by removing the iron with a magnet (3). When iron filings and sulfur are heated (4) they combine and change into iron sulfide, a compound.

Q What chemicals are used in fire extinguishers?

A Carbon dioxide extinguishers send out a jet of carbon dioxide gas. Dry powder extinguishers blanket a fire with powder. Soda-acid extinguishers (right) mix sulfuric acid with sodium carbonate, making carbon dioxide gas which forces out a jet of water.

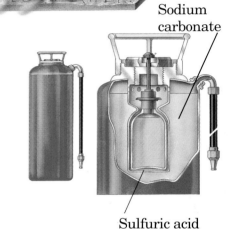

Sodium carbonate

Sulfuric acid

Q How do soaps and detergents work?

A Soaps and detergents are made from long molecules that are water-loving at one end and grease-loving at the other end. When they go to work on dirty cloth, they surround each droplet of greasy dirt stuck to the fibers of the cloth with their grease-loving tails plugged into the grease droplet (below). The coated droplet then floats off the cloth into the water and is washed away.

1   2

3   4

Grease

Cloth

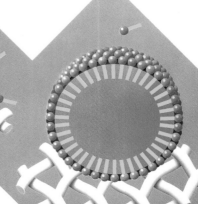

Q How are chemicals made?

A The chemical industry makes chemicals by processing raw materials with heat, pressure and chemical reactions. Sulfuric acid is made from sulfur in a series of stages (right) that change sulfur into different compounds, ending with sulfuric acid.

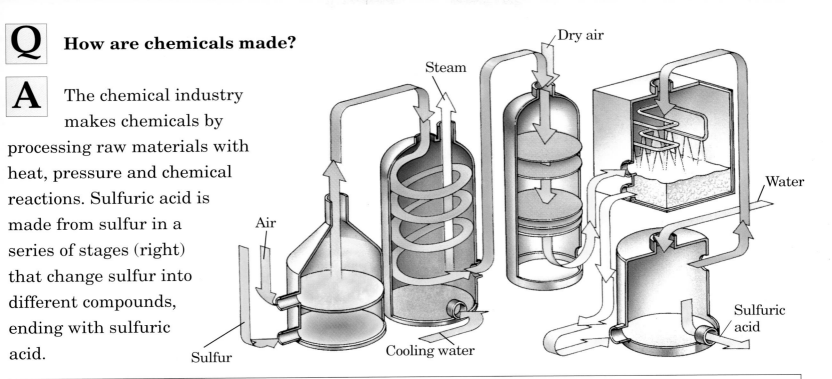

Steam

Dry air

Air

Water

Sulfur

Cooling water

Sulfuric acid

Q What are crystals?

A Crystals are solid pieces of material with flat faces set at angles to each other. All crystals of the same substance have the same angles between their faces. Crystals form in this way because their atoms always lie in the same regular patterns. Salt, sugar, and quartz are crystals. Minerals can sometimes be identified by the shape of their crystals.

Q What is chemical analysis?

A Chemists use chemical analysis (right) to find out what an unknown substance contains. There are several methods. Volumetric analysis involves reactions in solutions. Gravimetric analysis involves weighing. In gas-liquid chromatography gas carries the sample through a column of moist powder. The sample separates into simpler compounds which are recorded on a chart as they leave the column.

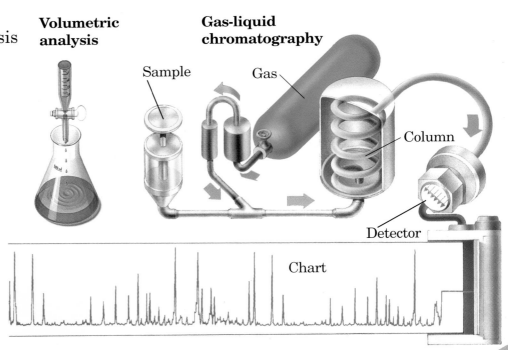

Volumetric analysis

Gas-liquid chromatography

Sample

Gas

Column

Detector

Chart

ATOMS & MOLECULES

Q What is inside an atom?

A An atom is made up of three kinds of tiny particles. Protons have a positive electric charge, and neutrons have no charge at all. Protons and neutrons cluster together at the center of the atom, making up the nucleus. Around them travel electrons, which have a negative electric charge. An atom contains equal numbers of electrons and protons.

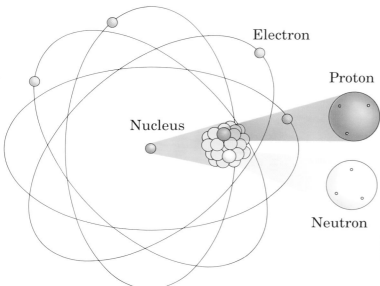

Electron

Nucleus

Proton

Neutron

Q How are atoms split?

A The atoms of different substances have different numbers of protons. Hydrogen has only one, but uranium has 92. All these protons jostle around, making uranium very unstable. If extra neutrons are fired into the atom's nucleus, they are absorbed. This splits the nucleus in two, releasing energy as heat, and extra neutrons (right).

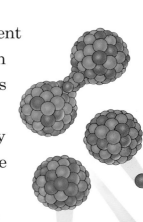

Proton

Neutron

Uranium nucleus

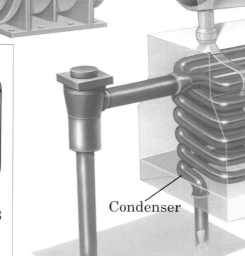

Generator

Turbine

Condenser

Q What happens when molecules are heated?

A If a solid object (1) is heated, its molecules vibrate strongly. If it gets hot enough, the solid melts into a liquid (2). Greater heat makes the liquid turn into gas (3).

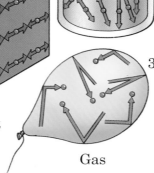

Solid object

1

Liquid

2

Gas

3

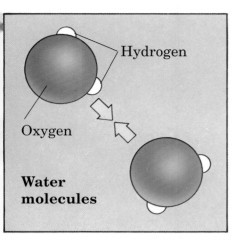

Hydrogen

Oxygen

Water molecules

Q What is a molecule?

A
A molecule is the smallest part of a substance. Its atoms are linked chemically. Two hydrogen atoms and one oxygen atom make a water molecule (left).

Q How can we use the energy from atoms?

A
When a uranium atom is split, it releases neutrons which shoot off into surrounding atoms and split them, too. This splitting keeps going in what is called a chain reaction. It gives out a lot of energy in the form of heat, which can be used to generate electricity in a nuclear power station (left). Rods of uranium are placed inside the reactor. Control rods made of boron are put between the uranium rods to control the reaction. Water is pumped through the reactor under pressure and absorbs the heat. This water is carried to the steam generator, where its heat is used to boil a separate supply of water into steam. The steam is fed to a turbine. It spins the turbine, which turns the generator and so produces electricity. The used steam then travels to the condenser, where it is turned back into water and fed back to the steam generator to be reused.

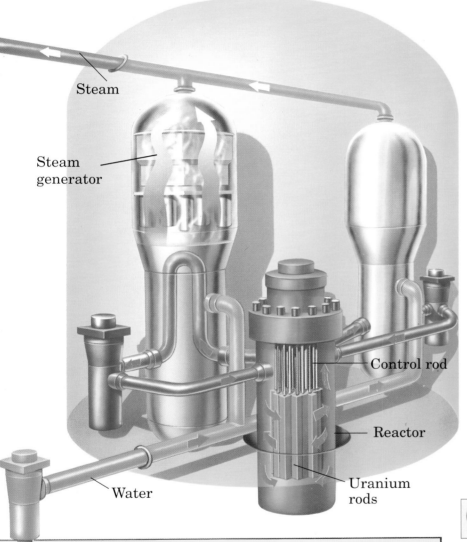

Steam

Steam generator

Control rod

Reactor

Uranium rods

Water

Q What types of radiation are there?

A
There are three types of radiation – alpha, beta, and gamma. Alpha particles are the least powerful. They cannot pass through paper. Beta particles cannot pass through thin metal, such as aluminum, and gamma rays cannot pass through lead (left).

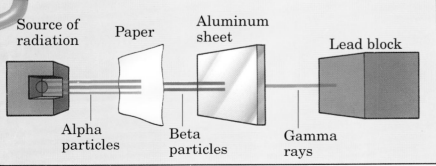

Source of radiation

Paper

Aluminum sheet

Lead block

Alpha particles

Beta particles

Gamma rays

SCIENCE & TECHNOLOGY

MATERIALS

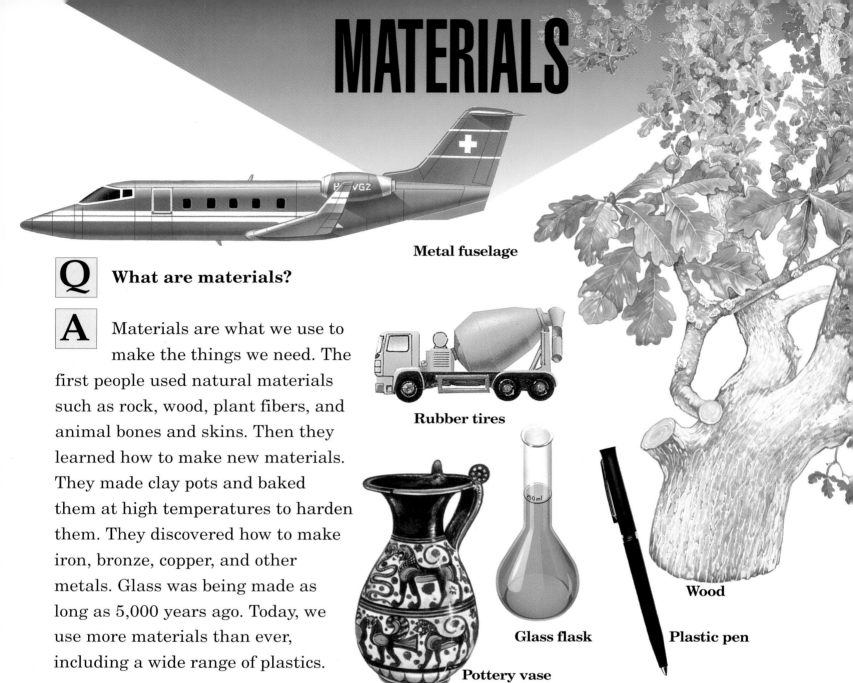

Metal fuselage

Rubber tires

Pottery vase

Glass flask

Plastic pen

Wood

Q What are materials?

A Materials are what we use to make the things we need. The first people used natural materials such as rock, wood, plant fibers, and animal bones and skins. Then they learned how to make new materials. They made clay pots and baked them at high temperatures to harden them. They discovered how to make iron, bronze, copper, and other metals. Glass was being made as long as 5,000 years ago. Today, we use more materials than ever, including a wide range of plastics.

Q What materials come from plants?

A People have used materials taken from plants since prehistoric times, and plants are still a very important source of materials today. Timber, resins, rubber, cotton, linen, dyes, essential oils, and a wide range of medicines are still obtained from plants.

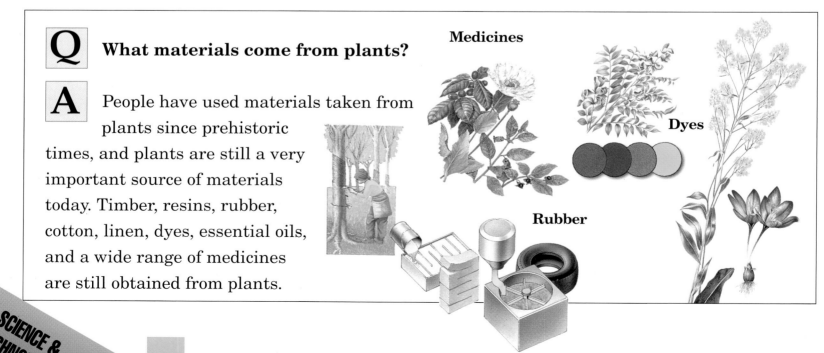

Medicines

Dyes

Rubber

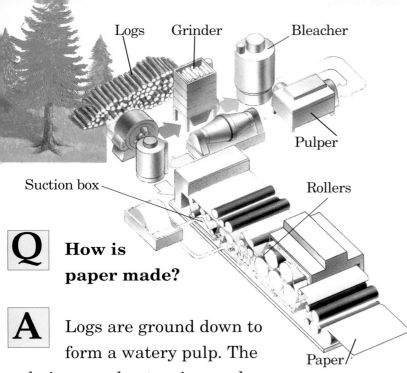

Logs Grinder Bleacher

Pulper

Suction box

Rollers

Q How is paper made?

Paper

A Logs are ground down to form a watery pulp. The pulp is poured onto wire mesh. Water is sucked and rolled out, leaving a thin film of paper. The process is continuous. Pulp is fed into one end of the machine (above) and paper comes out at the other end.

Q What are composites?

A Composites are materials made by combining two or more materials. Many kinds of boats (above) are made by laying mats of glass fibers into a mold and then soaking the mats in liquid plastic. The plastic sets hard and is reinforced by the fibers to make a smooth, tough, lightweight hull.

Q What do we get from crude oil?

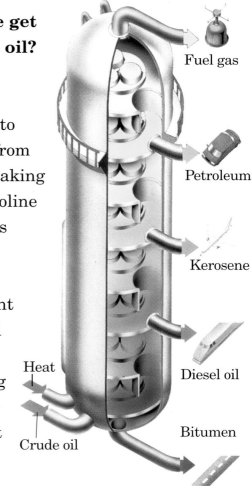

Fuel gas

Petroleum

Kerosene

Heat

Diesel oil

Crude oil

Bitumen

A Crude oil is separated into materials ranging from bitumen for road-making to fuels such as gasoline and gas. Crude oil is heated inside a tall fractionating tower (right). Gas and light fuels evaporate and collect near the top of the tower, leaving heavier oils and bitumen to settle at the bottom.

Q How is plastic recycled?

A Waste plastic is loaded into a furnace (below) and heated. The gas given off is then separated in a distillation column. Wax and tar collect at the bottom, while lighter gases collect further up. Some of the gas is fed back to fuel the furnace.

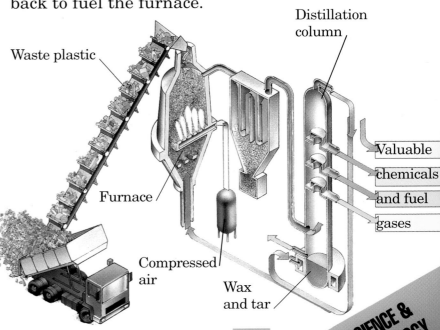

Waste plastic

Distillation column

Valuable chemicals and fuel gases

Furnace

Compressed air

Wax and tar

SCIENCE & TECHNOLOGY

FORCES & ENERGY

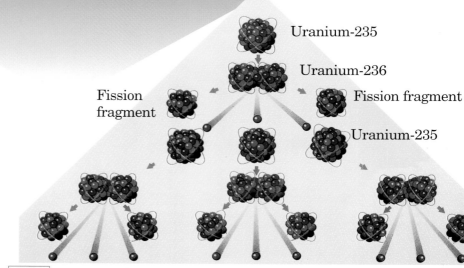

Slow-moving neutron

Uranium-235

Uranium-236

Fission fragment

Fission fragment

Uranium-235

Q What is gravity?

A Gravity is the force that pulls everything to Earth. Galileo showed that gravity makes all objects fall equally fast. When he dropped a light ball and a heavy ball from the leaning Tower of Pisa (above), they hit the ground at the same instant.

Q What is an Archimedes' Screw used for?

A The Archimedes' Screw (below) was invented by Archimedes in ancient Greece. It is used for lifting water. One end of the screw is dipped into water. By turning the handle, the water is raised up inside the tube until it spills out of the top.

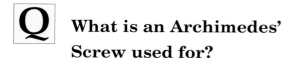

Q How is energy released inside a nuclear reactor?

A A slow-moving neutron is made to hit an atom of uranium-235 (above). It combines with the nucleus at the center of the atom, forming uranium-236. This splits into two particles called fission fragments, releasing a burst of energy and three more neutrons, which split more uranium atoms.

Q What forces act on an airplane in flight?

A Four forces act on an airplane. Its weight acts downward. The thrust of its engines pushes it forwards. Lift created by its wings acts upward. Drag tries to slow it down. Thrust must overcome drag, and lift must overcome weight, if a plane is to fly.

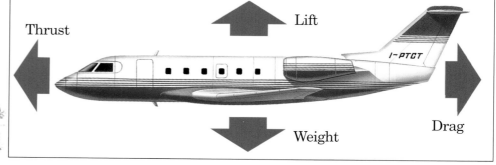

Thrust

Lift

Weight

Drag

Q How does a space rocket work?

A A rocket motor propels a rocket by burning fuel mixed with an oxidizer. The oxidizer contains oxygen, which is necessary for burning. The Ariane V rocket (below) burns hydrogen fuel with oxygen. The hot gas produced rushes out of the motor nozzles, forcing the rocket upward.

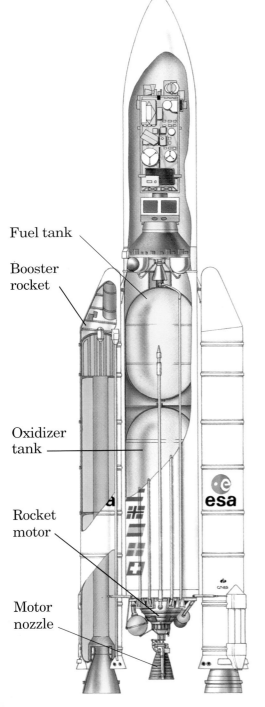

Fuel tank

Booster rocket

Oxidizer tank

Rocket motor

Motor nozzle

Q What is a force?

A A force is something that changes an object's speed or direction. Forces always exist in pairs acting in opposite directions. When a rifle is fired (below right), the rifle kicks back as the bullet flies forward. A heavier football player running faster applies a greater force than a lighter, slower player (below left).

Q What is friction?

A Friction is a force that stops surfaces from sliding across each other easily. Sometimes friction is helpful. It allows our shoes to grip the ground. Without friction walking would be impossible. But friction can also be a problem because it wears out the moving parts of machines.

Q How does a turbine work?

A A turbine (right) is a machine that uses gas or liquid to make a shaft turn. Water hitting the buckets of a Pelton wheel drives the buckets around and turns the shaft. Wind spins the blades of a wind turbine. Wind and water turbines often drive electricity generators.

Wind turbine

Rotor blade

Generator

Pelton wheel

Water jet

Shaft

Buckets

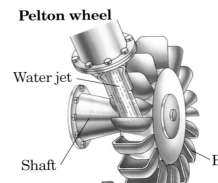

SCIENCE & TECHNOLOGY

SOUND

Direction of wave ➔

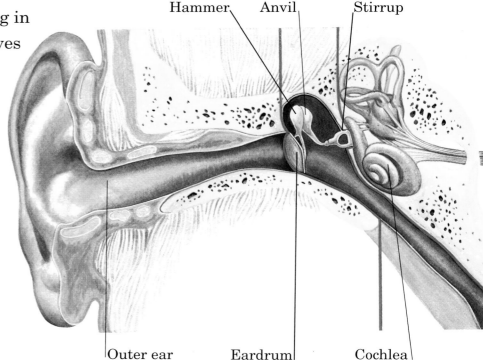

Rarefaction   Compression   Rarefaction

 Q   **What is sound?**

 A   Sound is a form of energy. Sound is made when something vibrates in air. The vibrations push against the surrounding air molecules, forming a sound wave. First the air molecules are squeezed (this is called compression), then they are stretched (this is called rarefaction). It is easiest to think of sound waves moving in the same way as a wave of energy moves along a coiled spring if one end is repeatedly pushed and pulled (above).

Q   **How do we hear sounds?**

A   When sound waves reach us, the outer ear channels them inside the ear, where they make the eardrum vibrate. The vibrations are magnified 20 times by the hammer, anvil, and stirrup bones, causing liquid to vibrate inside a tube called the cochlea (right). Nerves in the cochlea pass messages to the brain, enabling us to recognize the sound.

Hammer   Anvil   Stirrup

Outer ear   Eardrum   Cochlea

Q   **How fast does sound travel?**

A   Sound travels through solids, liquids, and gases at different speeds. Its speed depends on the density of the material. It travels faster through dense materials like steel than through less dense materials like air (below).

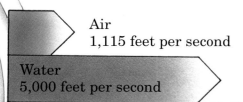

Air
1,115 feet per second

Water
5,000 feet per second

Concrete
16,000 feet per second

Steel
20,000 feet per second

Q How is loudness measured?

A Loudness depends on the amount of energy carried by a sound wave. The loudness of sound is measured in decibels (dB). Sounds louder than 120dB can damage the ears. Sounds louder than 130dB cause pain. Some animals, like bats, make sounds that we cannot hear at all (below).

Decibels 140   Pain threshold

130

100

70

40

0

Q Why does the sound of a racing car engine change as it drives past us?

A As the racing car (right) approaches, the sound waves in front of it get squashed together. These short sound waves make the engine's noise sound high-pitched. As the car moves past, the sound waves become stretched out behind it. The longer waves make the engine's note sound lower.

Q How does sound travel down telephone wires?

A A microphone in the mouthpiece converts the sound pressure waves of the caller's voice into electrical signals. These flow along wires (below) to the telephone at the other end. The magnet in the earpiece converts the signals back into sound pressure waves.

Magnet

Microphone

ELECTRICITY & MAGNETISM

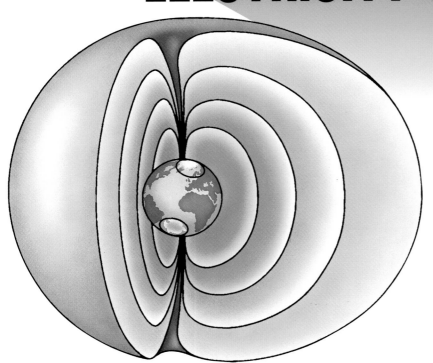

Q How do electric vehicles work?

A An electric car (above) works by using electricity stored in batteries to power an electric motor connected to the car's wheels. Electric trains are supplied with electricity from wires above the track or a third rail beside the track. It powers electric motors that turn the wheels.

Q What is a magnetic field?

A A magnetic field is a region of forces that exists around a magnet. The field can be drawn as a series of curved lines, called lines of force, joining the magnet's north and south poles. The Earth behaves like a magnet. Its magnetic field (above), caused by electric currents inside the liquid part of its core, stretches thousands of miles into space.

Q How are magnets made?

A An iron bar contains molecular magnets pointing in all directions. If the bar is placed inside a coil carrying an electric current, the molecular magnets line up with the coil's magnetic field. The bar has now become a magnet (right).

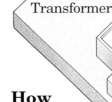

Power station

Transformer

Transmiss
tower

Q How do we get electricity?

A Electricity made at power stations (above) is distributed along cables at a very high voltage. The cables cross the countryside, strung between tall transmission towers. Electricity is distributed inside towns and cities by underground cables. Before it can be used, its voltage must be reduced. The final voltage varies from country to country.

Q How do electric motors work?

A An electric motor is made of a coil of wire inside a magnet. The coil is free to turn. When an electric current flows through the coil, it magnetizes the coil. This magnetic field pushes against the magnetic field produced by the surrounding magnet, and this makes the coil spin.

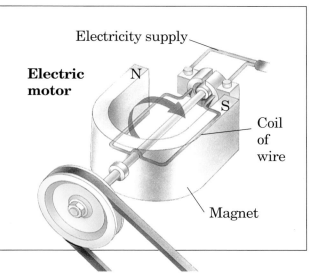

Electricity supply

Electric motor

N

S

Coil of wire

Magnet

Q How does a doorbell work?

A When the button (below) is pressed, the coil becomes magnetized. The iron rod shoots out of the coil and strikes the short chime. When the button is released, the rod swings back into the coil and hits the long chime.

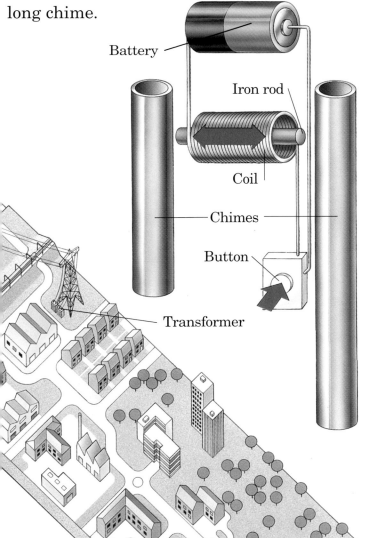

Battery

Iron rod

Coil

Chimes

Button

Transformer

Q What is inside a battery?

A Cars and trucks use a type of battery called a storage battery (below). It contains flat plates of lead and lead oxide dipped in sulfuric acid. When the battery is connected to a circuit, a chemical reaction between the plates and the acid makes an electric current flow around the circuit. A storage battery is recharged by passing an electric current through it.

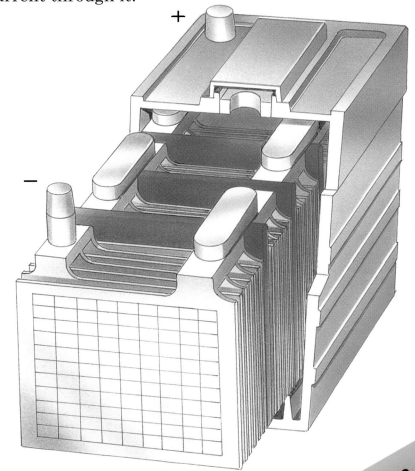

+

−

SCIENCE & TECHNOLOGY

HEAT & LIGHT

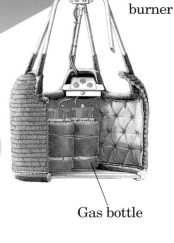

Gas burner

Q What is light?

A Light is a form of energy. It is composed of waves of electric and magnetic vibrations which our eyes can detect. The different colors (below) are produced by light waves of different lengths. We are unable to see waves shorter than blue light and longer than red.

Gas bottle

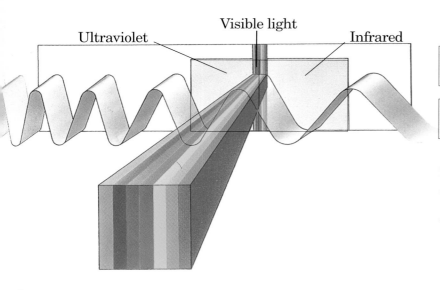

Ultraviolet   Visible light   Infrared

Q How does a hot-air balloon rise?

A A gas burner supplied with gas from bottles in the balloon's basket (above) heats the air inside the balloon. As the air warms up, it expands. The thinner air inside the balloon is lighter than the surrounding air, so the balloon floats upward.

Q How fast does light travel?

A The speed of light is 186,400 miles per second, faster than anything else in the universe. Light takes roughly 8.5 minutes to travel from the Sun (below) to the Earth. Looking at distant objects allows us to look back in time. When we look at a remote galaxy, we see it as it was when the light left it.

Q How does a laser work?

A Light is normally composed of different wavelengths (colors) mixed at random. A laser produces an intense beam of high-energy light in which all the light is of the same wavelength. The process is started by an electric current or a flash of light from a flash tube, which causes a gas or ruby rod (below) to send out the laser beam.

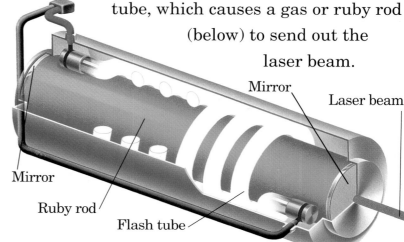

Mirror

Laser beam

Mirror

Ruby rod

Flash tube

Q What are thermals?

A Birds can often be seen gliding in tight circles, being carried upward by rising columns of air called thermals (right). Ground heated by the Sun warms the air above it. The warm air rises, sucking cool air in below it. That, too, is warmed and rises up. Glider pilots use thermals. They circle and climb inside one thermal, then glide to the next (below).

Bird's flight path

Thermal

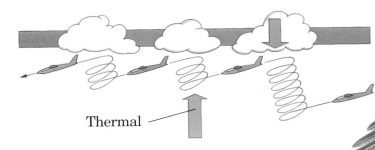

Thermal

Q How does a fluorescent tube work?

A A hot wire inside the tube sends out particles called electrons, which crash into atoms of mercury gas. The mercury atoms give out invisible ultraviolet radiation. The white phosphor coating inside the tube (below) changes this into bright visible light.

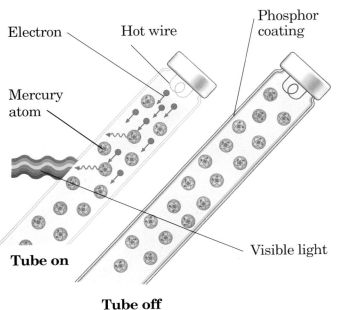

Electron   Hot wire   Phosphor coating

Mercury atom

Tube on

Visible light

Tube off

Q How does heat move along a metal bar?

A When something is heated, its atoms vibrate. If one end of a metal bar is heated, the atoms at that end vibrate more than the atoms at the cold end. The vibration spreads along the bar from atom to atom. The spread of heat in this way is called conduction. Metals are good conductors of heat.

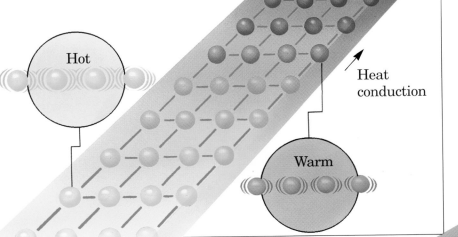

Cold

Hot

Warm

Heat conduction

SCIENCE & TECHNOLOGY

EVERYDAY SCIENCE

Q How does a digital watch work?

A Tiny quartz crystals inside the digital watch (right) vibrate at a steady rate when an electric current from a battery is applied. A silicon chip picks up the vibrations and turns them into regular pulses. The pulses are displayed as numbers on the liquid crystal display (LCD) on the watch face.

LCD

Vibration

Battery

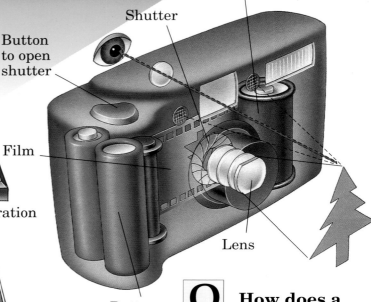

Film cassette

Shutter

Button to open shutter

Film

Lens

Battery

Q How does a camera work?

A When the camera's shutter is opened, light passes through a lens onto the film (above). The film is covered with chemicals that store the pattern as a photograph.

Fan

Electric motor

Elements

On/Off Switch

Q How do hair driers blow out hot air?

A A hair drier (above) uses electricity in two different ways. When you switch it on, a small electric motor turns a fan inside. The fan sucks in air from the back of the hair drier, and blows it out at the front. As the air travels through the hair drier, it passes over a set of wire coils called elements. These are heated by the electricity, warming the air as it passes.

Q How does a vacuum bottle keep liquids hot?

Cup

Stopper

A Inside a vacuum bottle are two glass bottles, one inside the other. They are sealed together at the top. The air between the two bottles is removed to form a vacuum. This helps to stop the heat escaping. The insides of the bottles are painted silver. This reflects the heat from the liquid inside the flask.

Vacuum

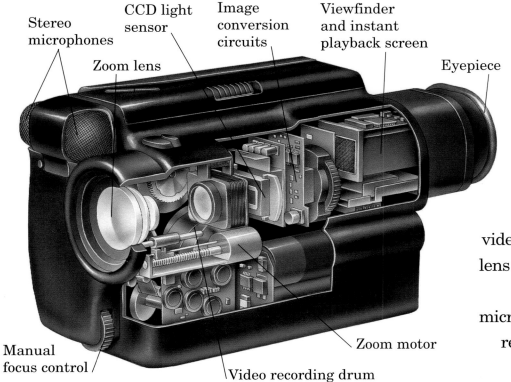

Stereo microphones

CCD light sensor

Image conversion circuits

Viewfinder and instant playback screen

Eyepiece

Zoom lens

Manual focus control

Video recording drum

Zoom motor

Q What is inside a video camera?

A Inside a video camera, a single charge coupled device (CCD) chip converts the image formed by the lens into a color video signal, which is recorded onto videotape. An infrared beam focuses the lens automatically, or the user can select manual focus. At the same time the microphones pick up the sound, which is recorded on the edge of the videotape.

Q Why do bicycles have gears?

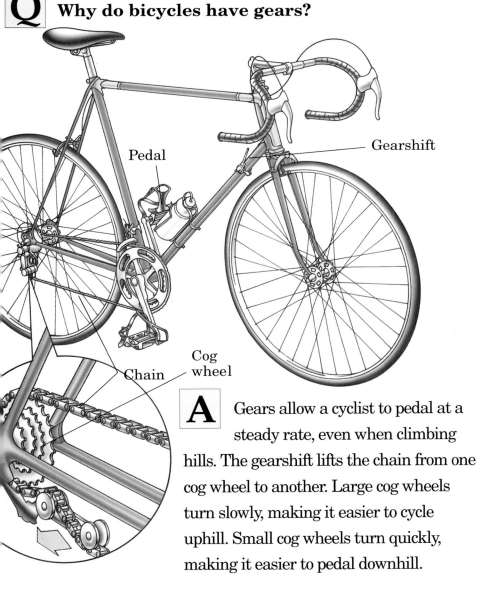

Gearshift

Pedal

Chain

Cog wheel

A Gears allow a cyclist to pedal at a steady rate, even when climbing hills. The gearshift lifts the chain from one cog wheel to another. Large cog wheels turn slowly, making it easier to cycle uphill. Small cog wheels turn quickly, making it easier to pedal downhill.

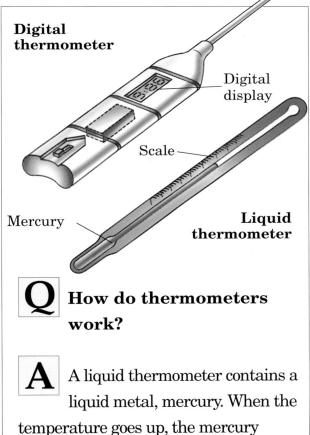

Digital thermometer

Digital display

Scale

Mercury

Liquid thermometer

Q How do thermometers work?

A A liquid thermometer contains a liquid metal, mercury. When the temperature goes up, the mercury expands and rises in the tube. A digital thermometer has an electronic circuit, which displays the temperature digitally.

INDUSTRY

Q How is plastic made into shapes?

A In blow molding, a piece of hot plastic tubing is placed in a mold. Air is blown into the tube, pushing it out into the shape of the mold.

Blow molding

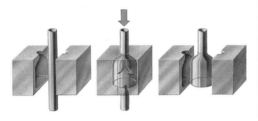

In vacuum molding, plastic is placed over a mold and heated. Air is removed, and the vacuum pulls the plastic into the mold.

Vacuum molding

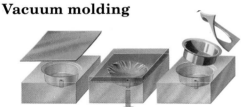

Q How is coal mined?

A Most coal is mined by either the "longwall" or "room-and-pillar" method (right). In longwall mining a giant coal cutter runs down the coal face removing coal as it goes. In room-and-pillar mining the coal is removed from chambers, but pillars of coal are left behind to support the roof.

Coal seam

Coal cutter

Longwall mining

Roof support

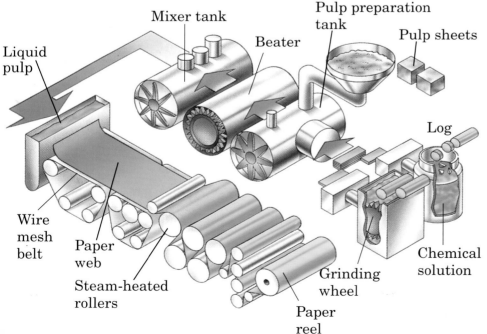

Mixer tank

Pulp preparation tank

Beater

Pulp sheets

Liquid pulp

Log

Wire mesh belt

Paper web

Steam-heated rollers

Grinding wheel

Chemical solution

Paper reel

Q What is paper made from?

A Most paper is made from wood (left). The wood is ground up or mashed into pulp using chemicals. The pulp is beaten so that the tiny wood fibers separate and soften. Then it passes onto a belt of wire mesh. The water drains through the mesh, and the pulp (now called the web) is squeezed first between heavy rollers and then between heated rollers. The dried and finished paper is wound onto reels.

Shaft

Ventilation shaft

Conveyor belt

Coal carried to surface

Q How is cloth made on a loom?

A A loom is a machine that joins together two yarns (long threads) in a crisscross pattern, to make a cloth. The warp yarn is strung along the loom (below). The threads are raised and lowered, forming a gap or "shed." Then a shuttle carrying the weft yarn is passed through the shed. Yarns can be woven into many different patterns.

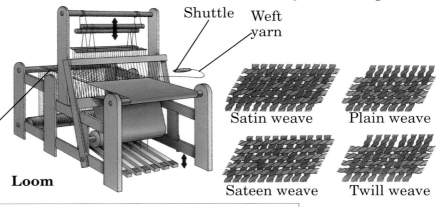

Shuttle

Weft yarn

Warp yarn

Loom

Satin weave

Plain weave

Sateen weave

Twill weave

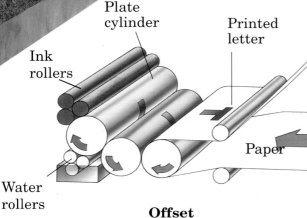

Plate cylinder

Printed letter

Ink rollers

Water rollers

Paper

Offset lithography

Q How is a newspaper printed?

A Each page is made into a metal plate, and wrapped around a cylinder. Where there are letters, chemicals allow ink, not water, to stick. A plate cylinder is inked and wetted, and the letters are printed on a roll of paper.

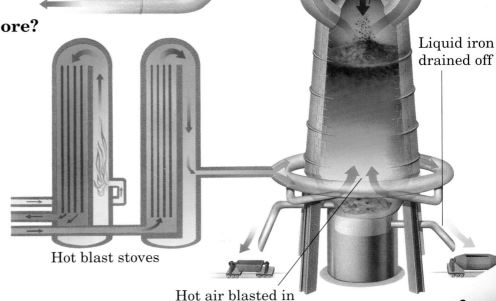

Iron ore mixed with limestone and coke

Liquid iron drained off

Hot blast stoves

Hot air blasted in

Q How is iron extracted from iron ore?

A Iron ore contains other substances besides iron. The iron is extracted in a tall tower called a blast furnace (right). The ore, mixed with limestone and coke, is fed through the top. Then very hot air is blown in through pipes at the bottom of the furnace. The iron melts, and the other materials rise to the top as slag. The iron is drained off from the bottom.

SCIENCE & TECHNOLOGY

TRANSPORTATION

Q What is a maglev train?

A Maglev trains are the trains of the future. They have been designed without wheels and use the principle of magnetic levitation to raise them off the track. With friction almost eliminated, they can be propelled forward at speeds of up to 250 mph. Prototypes of these "maglev" trains have already been built in Germany and Japan. In the future it is anticipated that maglevs will reach speeds of up to 500 mph.

Q How big is an oil tanker?

A Oil tankers (right) carry crude oil and oil products. Supertankers can carry hundreds of thousands of tons of oil. The largest supertanker was over 1,500 feet long and 226 feet wide. When it was fully loaded with petroleum, 79 feet of its hull were under water. Supertankers are difficult to steer, and so heavy that they can take up to three miles to stop completely.

Tug used to
help tanker dock

Q What is a tractor-trailer?

A A tractor-trailer (right) is one
that consists of two separate parts.
At the front is the part called the tractor
unit, which contains the diesel
engine, the controls, the fuel tank,
and the driver's cab. It has very
powerful brakes and some
have more than 20 gears.
The tractor unit pulls the
part called the trailer,
which carries the cargo.

Q What is a "supersonic" airliner?

A Supersonic means faster than the speed of sound.
The speed of sound is measured as 741 mph
at sea level. Concorde (left) is the only airliner
capable of flying at supersonic speed. It can
reach 1,350 mph. Other commercial aircraft
are not designed to fly at supersonic speed;
the shock waves and buffeting that would
occur as they approached
this speed would destroy
the aircraft.

Q Who built the first steam railway locomotive?

A In 1804, Richard Trevithick built the first successful steam
engine to run on rails. It hauled
trucks of coal along a tramway in
South Wales, UK. Trevithick
later built a locomotive called
'Catch me who can', which travelled
at speeds of up to 10 mph.

COMPUTERS

Q **What is a smart card?**

Microcircuit

A Smart cards (above) are used by banks and other organizations. Inside the small piece of plastic is a microcircuit on which information is stored. A smart credit card, for instance, has money values stored in it which are reduced every time a purchase is made. Prepaid phone cards are a simple form of smart card.

Q **Can robots do the same things as people?**

A Robots can perform many of the routine tasks carried out by people in factories and workshops (right). Different types of robot can be used for jobs such as welding or painting. Robots work without tiring, but can only repeat the task they have been programmed to perform.

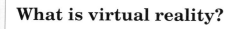

Pick-and-place robot

Q **What is virtual reality?**

A Virtual reality is a computerized fantasy world that seems like the real thing. To enter it, the user wears a helmet with a computer screen inside (right). As the user moves his/her head, different parts of the 'world' appear within the screen. In some virtual reality programs the user moves a joystick to make the images move on the screen. Sometimes sensors attached to the body enable the user to 'touch' things. The science of virtual reality is still at an early stage. It takes powerful computers to run even a simple program. Simulators used to train aircraft pilots and tank commanders use a form of virtual reality.

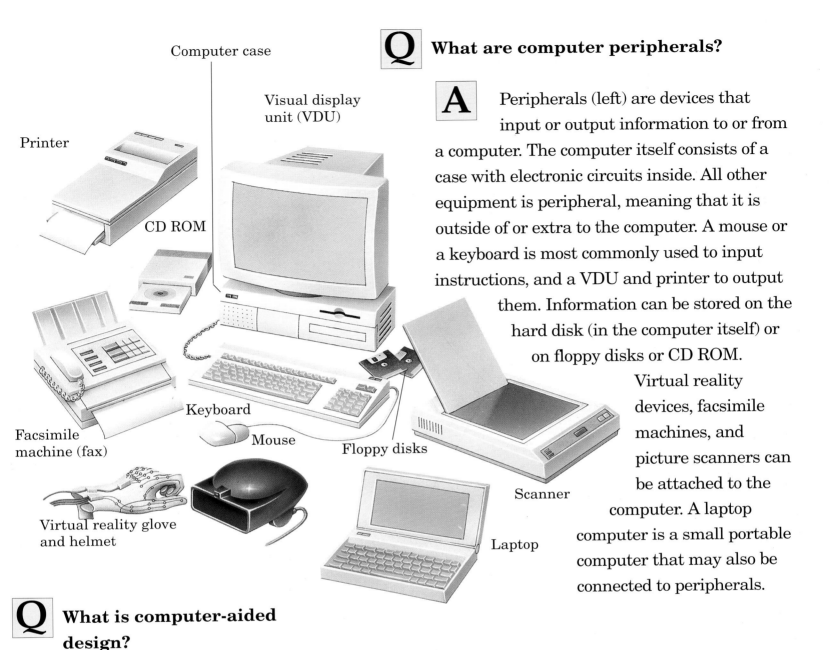

Printer

Computer case

Visual display unit (VDU)

CD ROM

Facsimile machine (fax)

Keyboard

Mouse

Floppy disks

Virtual reality glove and helmet

Laptop

Scanner

Q What are computer peripherals?

A Peripherals (left) are devices that input or output information to or from a computer. The computer itself consists of a case with electronic circuits inside. All other equipment is peripheral, meaning that it is outside of or extra to the computer. A mouse or a keyboard is most commonly used to input instructions, and a VDU and printer to output them. Information can be stored on the hard disk (in the computer itself) or on floppy disks or CD ROM.

Virtual reality devices, facsimile machines, and picture scanners can be attached to the computer. A laptop computer is a small portable computer that may also be connected to peripherals.

Q What is computer-aided design?

A Computer-aided design (CAD) is often used in industry. Details of a new product design are fed into a computer. The computer displays a model that designers can look at from all angles. They can test out new ideas on the model. For instance, the addition of a more powerful engine may require wider tires. Here (right) a computer model is being used to test air flow over a car design. This shows that the addition of a small spoiler on the rear of the car will give better road holding.

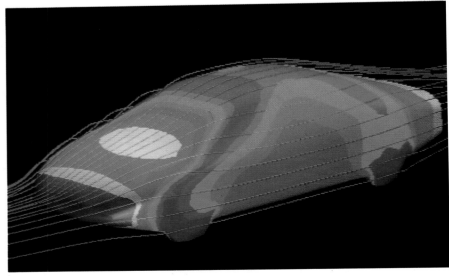

MACHINES

Q When was the first locomotive invented?

A On February 21, 1804, Richard Trevithick demonstrated his latest invention at the Penydarren mining railway in Wales. It was the world's first railway locomotive (right). It made a journey of 10 miles in four hours, pulling 11 tons of iron on which 70 men sat.

Q What is a bulldozer?

A A bulldozer is a machine used mainly on building sites to move earth. It has caterpillar tracks to grip soft ground and a blade at the front that can be raised or lowered. To scrape the ground level, the bulldozer drives forward with the blade lowered.

Q How does a hovercraft work?

A A hovercraft (below) travels over land and water by floating on top of a cushion of air. Powerful fans inside the hovercraft suck air down underneath it. A flexible rubber skirt around the edge of the hovercraft holds the air in as the craft rises. Propellers above the deck spin around to push the hovercraft forward.

Air

Fan

Propeller

Rubber skirt

Jib

Driver in cab

Weight to balance load

Q How does a tower crane work?

A A tower crane (right) moves materials on a building site. A hook is suspended from a trolley that can move along the jib. The jib can also swing around. The hook is raised by a motor which winds a cable around a drum. The open frame of the tower and jib saves weight.

Q How do machines study the Earth?

A Satellites orbiting the Earth are observing our planet all the time. Seasat (below) bounced radar signals off the sea to carry out oceanographic research. Other satellites measure the temperature of the sea and land, wind speed and direction, the height of waves, and pollution. They also measure forest clearance, iceberg movements, crop diseases, volcanic eruptions, and the ocean floor.

Radar signals

Sea surface

Seabed

Q How does a robot arm work?

A Robot arms are used in industry for cutting, drilling, welding, and painting. Their joints are driven by motors which are controlled by computer. Different tools can be fitted to the arm's mechanical hand and then its computer can be programmed to make it carry out different jobs.

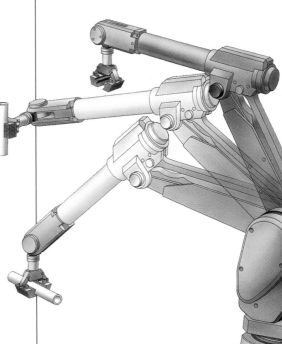

SCIENCE & TECHNOLOGY

SHIPS

GLOBTIK TOKYO

A The world's largest ships are cargo vessels. The largest of these are the supertankers that carry oil around the world (left). The oil tanker *Jahre Viking* was the largest ship afloat in 1999. It is 1,500 feet long and 226 feet across. Its cavernous hull extends 82 feet below the water-line. When it is fully loaded with crude oil, it weighs 621,500 tons.

Q How does a lifeboat work?

A When a distress message is received, a lifeboat is quickly on its way. It may be launched from a carriage, down a slipway, or from a permanent mooring that the crew reaches by small boat. Lifeboats are designed to operate in rough seas. Most can turn themselves the right way up if they capsize.

Q What is inside a submarine?

A A submarine (below) contains a pressurized compartment where the crew lives and works. The space between this and the outer hull contains a series of fuel, oil, water, waste, and ballast tanks. When the ballast tanks are flooded with sea water, the submarine becomes heavier than the surrounding water and sinks. When air is pumped into the tanks, forcing the water out, the submarine becomes lighter and rises.

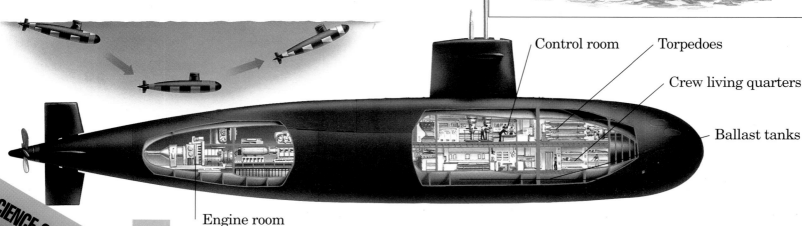

Control room   Torpedoes

Crew living quarters

Ballast tanks

Engine room

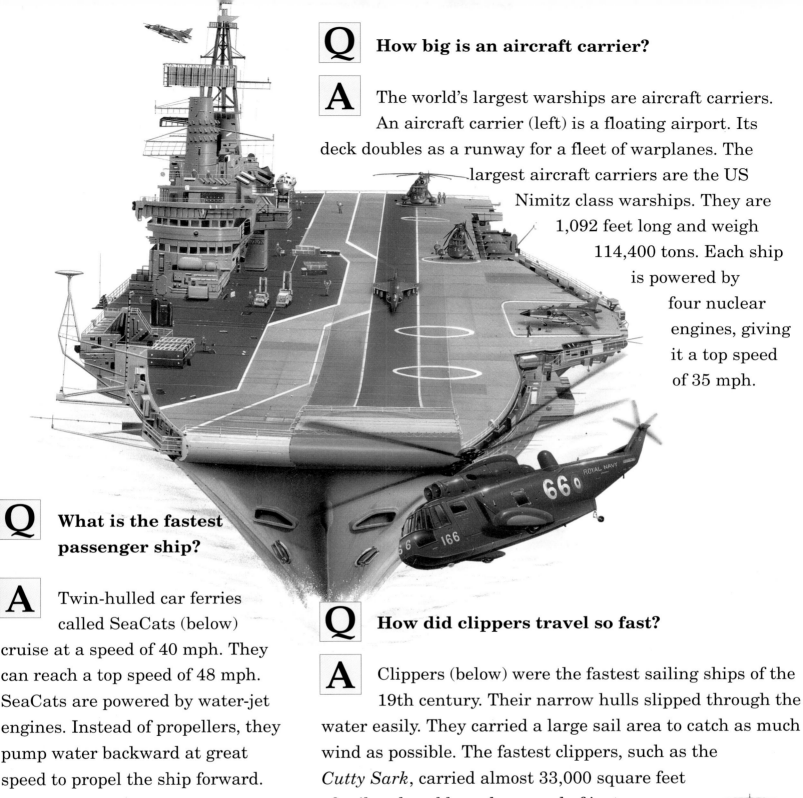

Q How big is an aircraft carrier?

A The world's largest warships are aircraft carriers. An aircraft carrier (left) is a floating airport. Its deck doubles as a runway for a fleet of warplanes. The largest aircraft carriers are the US Nimitz class warships. They are 1,092 feet long and weigh 114,400 tons. Each ship is powered by four nuclear engines, giving it a top speed of 35 mph.

Q What is the fastest passenger ship?

A Twin-hulled car ferries called SeaCats (below) cruise at a speed of 40 mph. They can reach a top speed of 48 mph. SeaCats are powered by water-jet engines. Instead of propellers, they pump water backward at great speed to propel the ship forward.

Q How did clippers travel so fast?

A Clippers (below) were the fastest sailing ships of the 19th century. Their narrow hulls slipped through the water easily. They carried a large sail area to catch as much wind as possible. The fastest clippers, such as the *Cutty Sark*, carried almost 33,000 square feet of sail and could reach a speed of just over 19 mph.

SCIENCE & TECHNOLOGY

UNDERSEA EXPLORATION

Q How did early diving suits work?

A Early diving equipment made in the 1600s and 1700s worked by pumping air down a hose from the surface into a metal helmet over the diver's head (right). The pressure of the air inside the helmet stopped water from rising up inside.

Q How does a pressurized diving suit work?

A A pressurized diving suit (below) is supplied with air pumped from the surface through a hose. The diver can change the air pressure inside the suit by adjusting a valve in the helmet. Heavy metal boots help keep the diver weighted down on the seabed.

Q What is an atmospheric diving suit?

A An atmospheric diving suit (below) is a watertight suit of armor used for the deepest dives. The diver breathes air at atmospheric pressure, which is that of surface air. The heavy metal suit with watertight joints stops the huge water pressure 1,000 feet below the surface from crushing it.

Q What is an aqualung?

A An aqualung (above) is a device that enables divers to move around freely under water without any connection with the surface. The diver breathes air from tanks worn on the back.

Q Why are shipwrecks explored?

A Sunken ships can tell us a lot about the sailors who sailed them and the world they lived in. The ship's timbers may be all that is left, but sometimes the divers who explore shipwrecks (right) find tools, guns, and some of the sailors' belongings.

Q What animals have been found in the ocean depths?

A Light does not reach the bottom of the ocean. Many of the fish that live there make their own light. They catch smaller fish by dangling a glowing lure over their mouth. Smaller fish swim toward the lure and straight into the fish's mouth.

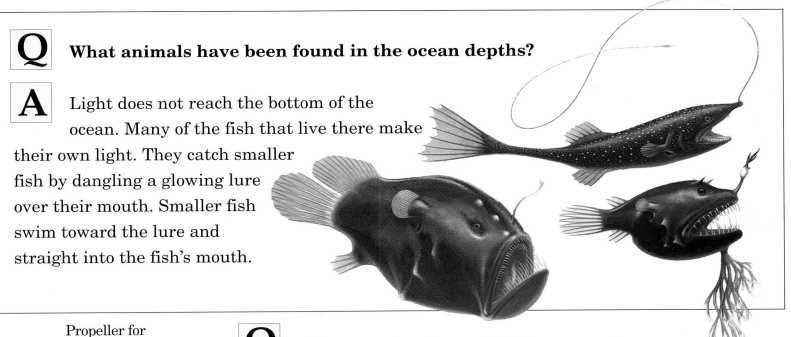

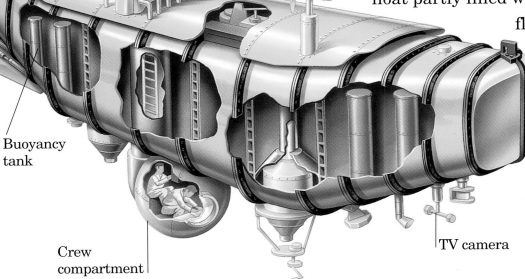

Propeller for maneuvering

Water ballast tank

Buoyancy tank

Crew compartment

Mechanical arm

TV camera

Q What was the deepest-diving vessel?

A On January 23, 1960, the bathyscaphe *Trieste* (left) descended 35,810 feet into the deepest part of the Mariana Trench in the Pacific Ocean. No one has dived deeper. *Trieste*'s crew of two were protected inside a thick metal sphere beneath a large float partly filled with gasoline. When sea water flooded into the float, *Trieste* sank. To return to the surface, it dropped metal weights.

SCIENCE & TECHNOLOGY

LAND TRAVEL

Q How are heavy loads carried by road?

A The largest and heaviest loads are carried on a special low trailer pulled by a powerful tractor unit (right). This vehicle has six axles to spread the load. The tractor unit has six sets of wheels. Four of them are driven by the engine to give maximum power.

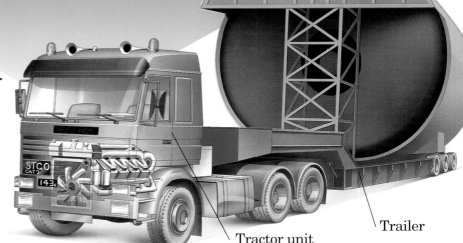

Tractor unit

Trailer

Q How does a refrigeration truck keep its cargo cold?

A Cargoes that have to be kept cold are transported in a refrigerated truck (below). The insulated trailer has a refrigeration unit on the front. Liquid coolant flows through pipes in the trailer and absorbs heat from the cargo. The coolant returns to the refrigeration unit and gives up its heat to the outside air. It is then compressed to turn it back into a cold liquid and recirculated through the trailer.

Refrigeration unit

Q Which were the largest steam trains ever?

A The largest steam locomotives ever built were five giants called Big Boys. They were built in the 1940s for the Union Pacific Railroad. The locomotive and its coal tender (right) were almost 130 feet long, 10 feet wide and 16 feet high. They each weighed 660 tons. They pulled up to 4,400 tons of freight in the Rocky Mountains.

Q Can the Sun power vehicles?

A Sunshine can be turned into electricity by solar cells. A vehicle covered with solar cells can produce enough electricity to drive an electric motor. A solar-powered bicycle crossed Australia at an average speed of 30 mph. The fastest solar-powered car, Sunraycer, was capable of a top speed of 48 mph.

Q What is the fastest train?

A The world's fastest train in service today is the French TGV (Train à Grande Vitesse) Atlantique. The first of these high-speed electric trains was introduced in 1981. On May 18, 1990, a TGV Atlantique train (right) reached the record-breaking speed of 320 mph between Courtalain and Tours. In everyday passenger service, TGV Atlantiques normally travel at up to 185 mph.

Q What is a supercar?

A Supercars are the super sedans and super sports models of the car world. They are fast, powerful, and very expensive. The Ferrari F40 (right) is certainly a supercar. One of the world's fastest production cars, it can reach a top speed of 200 mph. One special feature is that the engine is behind the driver.

CARS

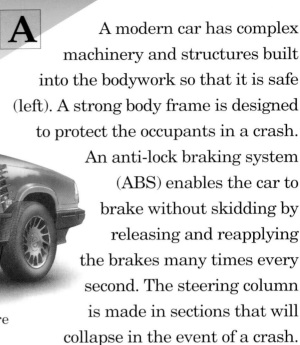

Q How is a modern car built for safety?

A A modern car has complex machinery and structures built into the bodywork so that it is safe (left). A strong body frame is designed to protect the occupants in a crash. An anti-lock braking system (ABS) enables the car to brake without skidding by releasing and reapplying the brakes many times every second. The steering column is made in sections that will collapse in the event of a crash.

Body frame

Steering column

Tire

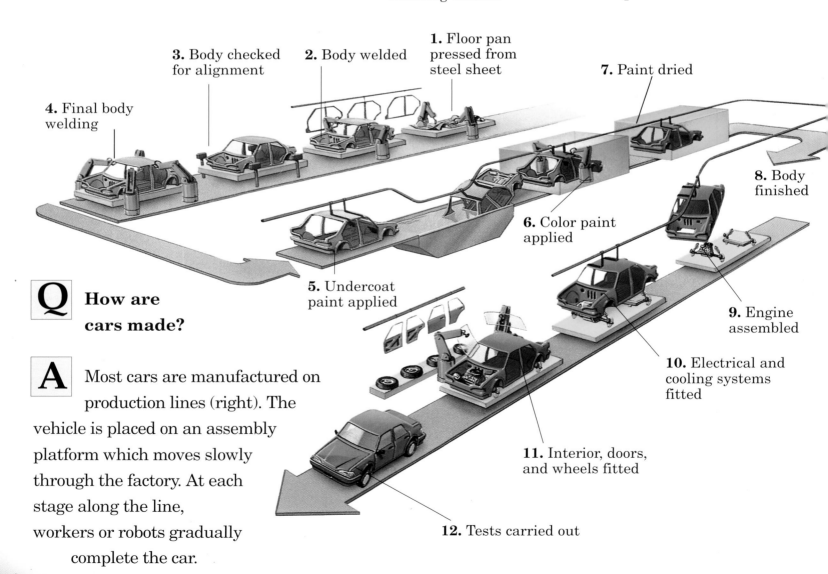

1. Floor pan pressed from steel sheet

2. Body welded

3. Body checked for alignment

4. Final body welding

5. Undercoat paint applied

6. Color paint applied

7. Paint dried

8. Body finished

9. Engine assembled

10. Electrical and cooling systems fitted

11. Interior, doors, and wheels fitted

12. Tests carried out

Q How are cars made?

A Most cars are manufactured on production lines (right). The vehicle is placed on an assembly platform which moves slowly through the factory. At each stage along the line, workers or robots gradually complete the car.

Q Why do car engines need oil?

A As a car travels, many of its parts move against each other. The different parts of the engine (right) move at high speed. Oil is pumped from the oil pan to lubricate the bearings, pistons, and other components, allowing the metal parts to move without causing wear or generating heat through friction. Some vehicles use special oils if they are to be used in very cold conditions.

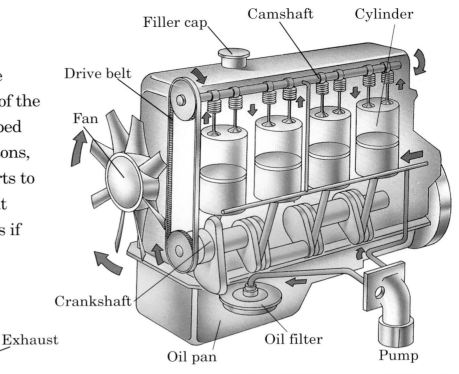

Filler cap · Camshaft · Cylinder
Drive belt
Fan
Crankshaft
Oil filter
Oil pan
Pump

Fuel in
Air in
Injector
Spark plug
Exhaust
Cylinder

Q What is fuel injection?

A Car engines burn fuel in closed cylinders. A fuel injection system pumps a precise amount of fuel into the cylinders as air is sucked in (above). The mixture is then ignited by a spark plug and the waste gases flow through the exhaust.

Q What did the first cars look like?

A The first cars were built in the 1880s. At first, engines were built into carriages normally pulled by horses. These "horseless carriages" had simple controls.

Q How are racing cars designed to go fast?

A Most modern cars are designed for comfortable travel. Racing cars (right), however, are designed for speed. They are very light, but strong, and the powerful engines are designed to accelerate extremely fast. The tires are wide, so they grip the road extremely well. The bodywork is designed to reduce air resistance, and special fins are added to improve handling and road holding.

Engine

Extra-wide tires

FLIGHT

Q How does an airplane stay in the air?

A Airplanes (left) can fly because of the shape of their wings. The top of the wing is more curved than the bottom. Air rushing over the top of the wings travels further and faster than the air flowing underneath. This produces lower air pressure above the wings than below them (below), causing the wings to lift.

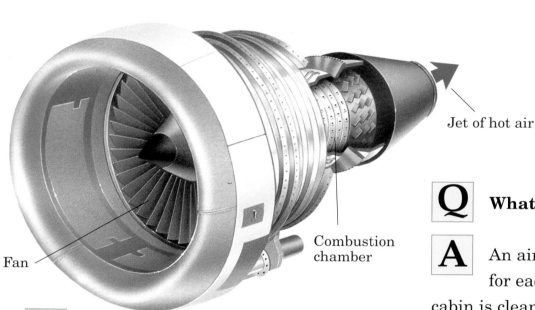

Fan

Combustion chamber

Jet of hot air

Air flow

Q How does a jet engine work?

A A large spinning fan at the front of the engine (above) sucks in air. The air is then compressed and heated by burning fuel in the combustion chamber. This makes the air expand quickly. A jet of hot air rushes out of the back of the engine and pushes the airplane forward.

Q What happens before takeoff?

A An airliner (below) is carefully prepared for each flight. The passenger cabin is cleaned. Meals and baggage are loaded. The fuel tanks are filled. Engineers check the plane and the crew does its preflight checks.

Q What did the first airplane look like?

A The first airplane, called *Flyer 1* (right), flew in 1903. It was made of wood. It had two wings covered with fabric, one above the other, and the pilot lay down on the lower wing to fly it.

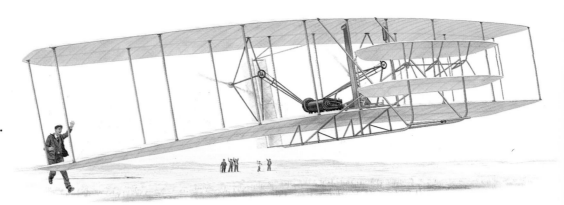

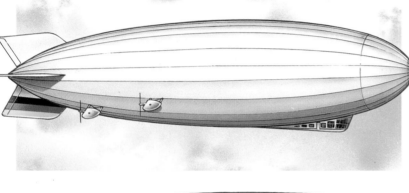

Hindenberg 800 feet

Concorde 204 feet

Q What is a Zeppelin?

A A Zeppelin (left) is a giant airship named after its inventor, Count Ferdinand von Zeppelin. The Zeppelins were built in Germany between 1900 and the 1930s. The biggest passenger-carrying Zeppelins were the *Graf Zeppelin* and the *Hindenberg*. They carried passengers across the Atlantic Ocean. Zeppelins could fly without wings because they were filled with hydrogen gas. This is lighter than air and made the airships float upward.

Q Which aircraft can carry the largest cargo?

A The Airbus Super Transporter A300-600ST Beluga has the largest cargo of any aircraft. It can carry up to 50 tons of cargo in a hold that is 121 feet long and up to 24 feet wide. Belugas are built from Airbus A300 airliners. They replaced the Super Guppy transporter (below). The Super Guppies were built to transport parts of the giant Saturn 5 moon rockets.

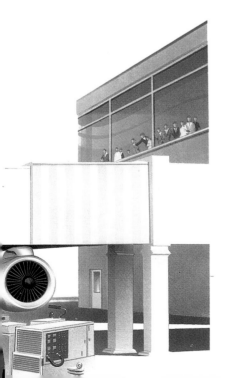

AIRBUS SKYLINK

SCIENCE & TECHNOLOGY

STRUCTURES

Q How long did it take to build the Great Pyramid?

A The Great Pyramid was built as a tomb for King Khufu, also called Cheops. It is at Giza, in Egypt. Work began in about 2575 BC. It took thousands of people about 25 years to assemble it (right) from 2.3 million blocks of stone. It weighs over 6.6 million tons and is today 450 feet high. The Great Pyramid was the tallest building in the world for 4,000 years.

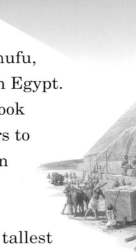

Entrance

Burial chamber

Q What type of bridge is the Sydney Harbor Bridge?

A The Sydney Harbor Bridge in Australia is a steel arch bridge spanning 1,650 feet. It is not the longest steel arch, but it is the widest. It carries two railroad tracks, eight traffic lanes, a bicycle path and a footpath. It was opened in 1932.

Q What is the Eiffel Tower?

A The Eiffel Tower (right) is one of the most famous French landmarks. Designed by the engineer Alexandre-Gustave Eiffel, it was built in 1889 to celebrate the 100th anniversary of the French Revolution. It stands 1,000 feet high, and is a slender pyramid made from 7,700 tons of iron girders.

Q How is the space shuttle moved to its launch pad?

A The space shuttle (left) is prepared for launch inside a building at the Kennedy Space Center in Florida. It is moved to the launch pad four miles away by the world's largest crawler transporter. This giant is 130 feet long and weighs 3,000 tons. It travels on four double caterpillar tracks. The tracks are moved by electric motors driven by generators powered by diesel engines.

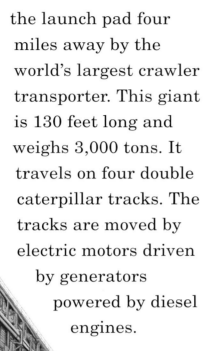

Q What is an oil platform?

A Oil platforms are offshore drilling rigs that stand on the seabed. The tallest is the Auger platform in the Gulf of Mexico. It stands in 2,860 feet of water. The Gullfaks C platform (above) in the North Sea stands on concrete pillars and supports production equipment, loading derricks, and a helicopter pad.

Q How does a flood barrier work?

A The Thames Barrier (right) was opened in 1984 to protect London from flooding. It consists of eight gates, each weighing 4,000 tons. They normally lie on the riverbed. If there is any danger of flooding, the gates are rotated to raise them up against the flood water.

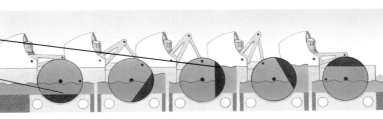

Gate raised

Gate lowered

SCIENCE & TECHNOLOGY

BUILDINGS

Q Why was the Great Wall of China built?

A The Great Wall of China (right) was built by Chinese emperors to keep out invaders. Most of it was built by the emperor Shih Huang Ti between 221 BC and 204 BC. The wall finally reached a length of about 4,000 miles. Much of the wall is still standing.

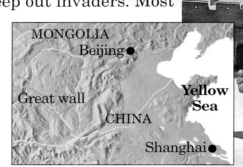

MONGOLIA
Beijing●

Great wall

CHINA

Yellow Sea

Shanghai●

Q What is Abu Simbel?

A Abu Simbel is a place in Egypt where the Egyptian king, Rameses II, built two temples in about 1250 BC. They were cut into blocks and rebuilt on higher ground in the 1960s when the rising waters of Lake Nasser threatened to cover them.

Q Which building materials did the Romans use?

A Most Roman buildings (right) were made of bricks and concrete. Stone and glass were more expensive, so they were only used for important buildings. Romans were experts at building arches. They built a temporary wooden arch first, then covered it with bricks and poured concrete over the top. Finally the wooden arch was removed.

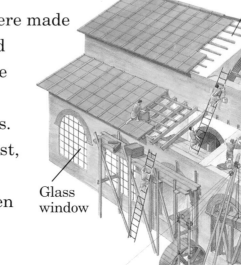

Concrete

Bricks

Wooden arch

Glass window

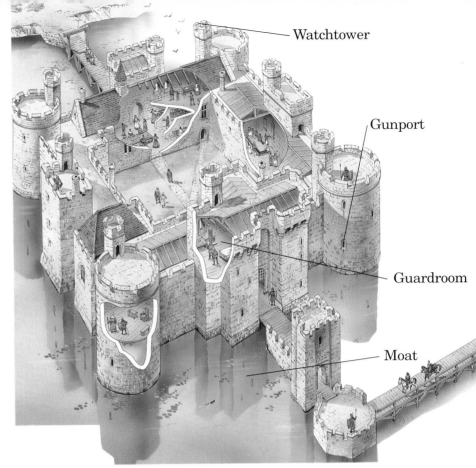

Watchtower

Gunport

Guardroom

Moat

Q Why were castles built?

A Castles were built to protect the people who lived in them. They were often built on hilltops or surrounded by water to make them easier to defend. Bodiam Castle (right) was a manor house in Sussex, England, that was strengthened to resist French attacks in the 1300s.

Q Why was the Statue of Liberty built?

A The Statue of Liberty (above) stands on an island at the entrance to New York Harbor. It was a gift from France to the USA in 1886 to celebrate the American Revolution. It is made of copper sheeting, and with its base stands 302 feet high. Its rusting iron skeleton was replaced by stainless steel in the 1980s.

Q What is a skyscraper?

A A skyscraper is a very tall building supported by a steel frame inside it. The world's most famous skyscraper is the Empire State Building in New York (right). Built in 1931, it stands 1,250 feet tall. The tallest skyscrapers today are the twin Petronas Towers in Malaysia. They stand 1,483 feet high, 483 feet taller than the Eiffel Tower in Paris, France, which was itself the tallest building in the world until 1930.

Eiffel Tower

Empire State Building

Petronas Towers

SCIENCE & TECHNOLOGY

FARMING

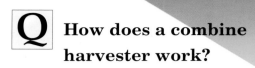

Q How does a combine harvester work?

A A combine harvester (right) does nearly all the jobs in harvesting a cereal crop. At the front is the big pick-up reel. This pulls the crop into the cutter bar. The cut cereal is pushed by a rotating screw onto an elevator, which takes it to the threshing area. This rotates very fast and separates the grain from the stalks. The grain is stored in a bin. When the bin is full, the grain is unloaded into a truck. The stalks are pushed out of the back of the harvester onto the ground.

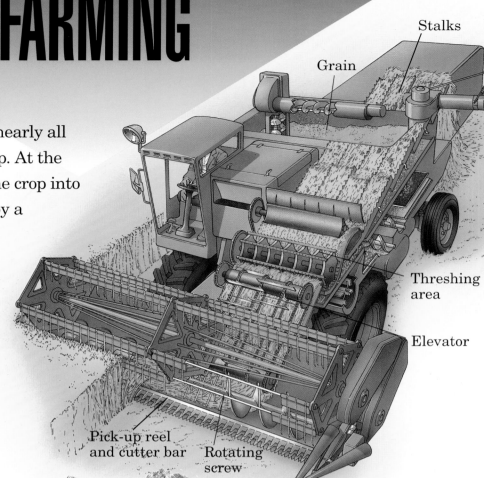

Stalks

Grain

Threshing area

Elevator

Pick-up reel and cutter bar

Rotating screw

Rye

Oats

Barley

Corn

Wheat

Rice

Sorghum

Millet

Q Which plants are the most important source of food?

A Cereals are plants that produce grains (above). They are our most important source of food. The most common cereal is wheat. It is used to make bread or pasta and is the staple food of more than a third of the world's people. Rye, oats, and barley are grown in northern Europe, mainly as animal food. Corn (maize) is a major crop in America and Africa, and rice is the staple grain of Asia. Sorghum and millet are also grown in Asia and Africa.

Q What is the cotton plant used for?

A The cotton plant grows in many of the warm parts of the world. The fibers that grow around the seeds are used to make cloth. The seeds are crushed to produce vegetable oil, or to make cattle food or fertilizers.

Q Why are there so many types of cattle?

A There are more than 200 breeds of cattle throughout the world. Many, such as this Friesian cow (right), are kept in herds to produce milk. Others, such as the Hereford, are raised for their meat. The hardy Zebu is best suited to the hottest parts of India and Africa.

Q Which products are made from milk?

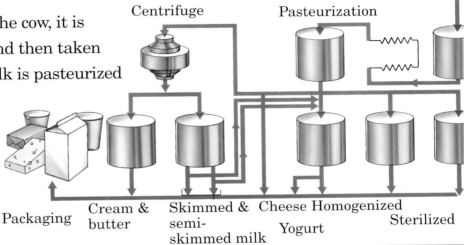

Cow   Farm vat   Tanker
Centrifuge   Pasteurization

A Milk has many uses. From the cow, it is pumped into the farm vat and then taken by tanker to the dairy. Here the milk is pasteurized (heated to kill the bacteria). If it is to be used for drinking, it is sealed into bottles or cartons. Milk can also be processed and turned into yogurt, cheese, cream, and butter.

Packaging   Cream & butter   Skimmed & semi-skimmed milk   Cheese   Homogenized Yogurt   Sterilized   UHT

Q Which fruits grow in tropical areas?

A Tropical regions are hot all year round. Here are some of the fruits that grow in these areas.
1. Pineapple, 2. Durian, 3. Carambola, 4. Mango, 5. Papaya, 6. Soursop, 7. Persimmon, 8. Mangosteen, 9. Pomegranate, 10. Litchi, 11. Akee, 12. Chirimoya, 13. Banana, 14. Guava, 15. Sapodilla, 16. Passion fruit, 17. Loquat, 18. Cape Gooseberry, 19. Rambutan.

Q Which countries have the most sheep?

A Australia is the biggest producer of sheep and wool in the world. In fact the country contains more sheep (about 156 million) than human beings. New Zealand is another major sheep producer, and contains about 20 sheep for every person! Many sheep are raised on the flat grasslands of South Africa, Argentina, and Uruguay, as well as in China and India. Altogether, there are about 1.1 billion sheep farmed throughout the world.

SCIENCE & TECHNOLOGY

INDEX